Count the Ways

To: Mom
From: Brad
August 9, 2002

Happy Birthday!

Count the Ways

THE GREATEST LOVE STORIES OF OUR TIMES

PAUL ARON

Contemporary Books

Chicago   New York   San Francisco   Lisbon   London   Madrid   Mexico City
Milan   New Delhi   San Juan   Seoul   Singapore   Sydney   Toronto

Library of Congress Cataloging-in-Publication Data

Aron, Paul.
    Count the ways : the greatest love stories of our times / Paul Aron.
       p.   cm.
    ISBN 0-07-138174-0
    1. Man-woman relationships—Case studies.   2. Mate selection—Case studies.
  3. Love—Case studies.   4. Courtship—Case studies.   I. Title.

    HQ801.A2 A76   2002
    306.7—dc21   2001047166

Contemporary Books

A Division of The **McGraw-Hill** Companies

  2 3 4 5 6 7 8 9 0 LBM/LBM 0 9 8 7 6 5 4 3 2

ISBN 0-07-138174-0

This book was set in Apollo
Printed and bound by Lake Book Manufacturing

Interior design by Monica Baziuk
Interior photographs copyright ©: New York World-Telegram & Sun: pp. 3, 27, 39, 61, 83, 143. Library of Congress: pp. 15, 105, 117, 131, 171, 193, 227, 241, 279. Corbis: pp. 51, 71, 157, 183, 217, 255, 267. Christopher Reeve Paralysis Foundation: p. 93. Pollock-Krasner House: p. 205.

McGraw-Hill books are available at special quantity discounts to use as premiums and sales promotions, or for use in corporate training programs. For more information, please write to the Director of Special Sales, Professional Publishing, McGraw-Hill, Two Penn Plaza, New York, NY 10121-2298. Or contact your local bookstore.

Contents

Barnstormers, Bank Robbers, and Ballplayers

❦— —❦

Preface

AT THIRTY-NINE, Elizabeth Barrett was an invalid, largely confined to her room, and completely under the sway of a tyrannical father who had prohibited any of his children from marrying.

Then, out of the blue, came a letter from her fellow poet, Robert Browning.

"I love your verses with all my heart, dear Miss Barrett," wrote Browning. He added: "And I love you, too."

They met a few months later and, to circumvent her father's ban, married in secret. Robert swept Elizabeth off to Pisa, where the climate worked miracles on her health. She had a child and became the poet of Italy's movement for national unification.

No wonder she loved her husband. "How do I love thee?" she wrote. "Let me count the ways."

And yet, as deeply as Elizabeth Barrett Browning loved Robert Browning, she could barely begin to count the multitude of ways in which people have loved. Indeed, her own story, though true, sounds a bit like a fairy tale, perhaps the narrowest of bands in the spectrum of love.

It's the contention of this book that there are more kinds of love than any one writer, even Browning, could possibly imagine. Here, for example, are Edith and Woodrow Wilson, for whom love was her path to power . . . and Edward VIII and Wallis Simpson, for whom love meant his giving up the throne. Here are Lee Krasner and Jackson Pollock, whose love kept him sane . . . and Scott and Zelda Fitzgerald, whose love drove her crazy. Here are Christopher and Dana Reeve, whose love inspired him to live . . . and Bonnie Parker and Clyde Barrow, for whom it meant certain death.

This book presents twenty-four loves from across the spectrum: some married and some not, some full of sexual passion and some not, some lasting and some not. Yet certainly this book is no more able than Elizabeth Barrett Browning to count *all* the ways of love.

Why, then, these of all the love stories that could be told?

One answer is that these are the stories that have most fully captured our attention over the last hundred years or so. The whole world, it seemed, was watching when Charles and Anne Lindbergh took off together, or when Joe DiMaggio, as one reporter put it, looked over Marilyn Monroe's curves.

Another answer is that, in spite of all that attention, the *true* stories of the couples in this book have often remained unknown. While fans were quick to blame Yoko Ono for breaking up the Beatles, few tried to understand what she and John Lennon felt for each other. And while the whole world focused on the disastrous marriage of Prince Charles and Lady Diana Spencer, few paid attention to his more lasting relationship with Camilla Parker Bowles (at least until the prince infamously expressed his desire to be her tampon).

Love stories, too often, are reduced to storybook romance—or to scandal. Which is a shame, because the true stories often turn out to be more romantic and always much richer.

These are, after all, the greatest love stories of our times.

Acknowledgments

As always, it has been a great pleasure to work with my editor, Judith McCarthy. Thanks also to Monica Baziuk, Michele Pezzuti, and Ellen Vinz of Contemporary Books, W. C. O'Donovan and Rusty Carter of the *Virginia Gazette*, and John Thornton of the Spieler Agency. Finally, thanks to Marilyn Aron, Thomas Aron, Liz Barnes, Tom Heacox, Suzanne Raitt, and especially Jae Aron and Paula Blank.

ACTORS AND ACTRESSES

Gracie Allen
and George Burns

*W*hen Gracie Allen and George Burns first teamed up for a new vaudeville act—in Newark, New Jersey, in 1923—they walked to center stage, hand in hand. Then Gracie dropped George's hand and walked toward a handsome man near the wings. She embraced and kissed him. Next Gracie walked back to center stage and asked George, "Who was that?"

The audience laughed.

"Gracie," George said, "you kiss a man, and you don't know who he is?"

And Gracie explained, "Mother told me never to talk to strangers."

The audience roared, and George and Gracie were on their way to stardom. She would play the same mixed-up but supremely self-confident character on radio and television, and George would continue to drolly puff his cigar and marvel at what he called Gracie's "illogical logic."

At twenty-five, George was already a show biz veteran, having been a part of almost fifty second-rate vaudeville teams. His real name was Nathan Birnbaum, but he was happy with any name that got him on the stage. Recalled George: "I was Glide of Goldie, Fields, and Glide; I was Jed Jackson of Jackson and Malone; I was Maurice Valente of Maurice Valente and His Wonder Dog; Harris of Harris and Dunlop; Jose of Jose and Dolores; at various times I was both Brown and Williams of Brown and Williams." He also worked with a trained seal.

He had even gone so far as to marry a dancer named Hannah Siegel, because her parents wouldn't let her tour with him unless they were married. The marriage, like the tour, lasted twenty-six weeks.

But with Gracie, George finally hit the big time. "Every time I looked at Gracie," he said, "I realized I'd finally found the thing I'd been searching for my whole life—a good act."

And, at least in part because of that, George fell in love with Gracie. "She was pretty, smart, nice, and talented," he said. "But I'll tell you the truth. I also fell in love with Gracie because I fell in love with making a good living."

The problem was, Gracie was already engaged. Her fiancé was Benny Ryan, a dancer also touring on the vaudeville circuit. Understandably, George was worried: "If she had married Benny Ryan, what was I going to do for an act? I had no real affection for the seal."

❦—❧

Like George, Gracie had started in show business as a child, touring with her sisters as part of a dancing quartet. But she was less committed to vaudeville than George, and when her sisters quit the act, she enrolled in stenography school. Still, she wasn't very enthusiastic about being a secretary either, so when a friend told her that George was looking for a partner, she agreed to give it a try.

Their first performance was a flop. George, intent on becoming a big-time comic, had given himself the punch lines. But the only laughter came for Gracie, who was supposed to be doing the straight lines. "I didn't have to be a genius to understand that there was something wrong with a comedy act when the straight lines got more laughs than the punch lines," George recalled. "So between the first and second show I decided to give Gracie a few of my toppers, just to see how the audience reacted."

By the time they finished their three-day run in Newark, Gracie had most of the punch lines and the audience loved her. "The audience created Gracie's character," George explained. "I listened to the jokes they laughed at and gave Gracie more of that type."

Of course, Gracie was neither the first nor the last to play a ditzy woman, or as they were then known, a "Dumb Dora." What made her special was that she delivered her lines not as punch lines, but as if they made complete sense. Somehow, when Gracie said them, they almost started to make sense to the audience too.

After Newark, the "Burns and Allen" act went on tour; they weren't yet in the big time, but they were no longer small time. They were making more money and doing fewer shows. There was still, however, the matter of Gracie's engagement to Benny Ryan.

At first, George courted her subtly, taking her dancing in the evenings. One advantage of this approach was that George was a very good dancer; after all, it had often been a part of his act.

The crisis came in 1925 when Ryan returned from a long tour expecting to marry Gracie. Ryan had a great deal going for him. "He was a tremendous talent, one of our top songwriters, a great dancer, an exciting performer," George admitted. "And besides that, he and Gracie had a lot in common. They were both Irish, they were both Catholic, and they both had their own hair.

"Gracie was a practicing Irish Catholic," he quipped. "I was Jewish, but I was out of practice."

The Orpheum vaudeville circuit rescued George by offering the team of Burns and Allen a whopping $450 a week. Gracie agreed to go on a new tour, and that gave George a chance to propose—nightly.

Eventually, on Christmas Eve 1925, she agreed. That was also the first night they slept together. A few weeks later, they took time off between shows in Cleveland and were married.

In one of their vaudeville routines, George asked Gracie whether the maid had dropped her on her head when she was a baby.

"Don't be silly, George," she answered. "We couldn't afford a maid. My mother had to do it."

Was the real Gracie so dizzyingly dumb? George would always insist that she was not. "She was very smart," he said. "Smart enough to become the dumbest woman in show business history."

But there's no question that her character drew on some of her actual characteristics, albeit in a much exaggerated form. For example, Gracie didn't handle money well, and her character once bragged that she had doubled the interest she got on her money by keeping it in two banks. Gracie was a lousy driver—she once suggested petitioning for more streetlights in Beverly Hills until someone pointed out she hadn't turned on her car lights. But she did not, as her character did, drive with her emergency brake on so she'd be ready for an emergency. Gracie wasn't much of a cook, especially because she spent so much time at work. But she did not insist, as her character did, that mathematicians were wrong because everyone knows that crackers can be squared but pi are round.

As for George, in spite of his many books of memoirs, the line between his act and his life was also difficult to discern—especially because the act was such an important part of his life. He could turn almost any recollection into a joke. When speaking of a brief affair he had with a starlet (he didn't name her) in the 1950s, for example, George said, "It was easy to have an affair in Hollywood. Even Lassie had puppies."

The affair took place after (though certainly not because) George and Gracie had fought about a silver centerpiece—she wanted to buy it, he didn't. After a few days, feeling tremendously guilty, George bought her the centerpiece along with a diamond ring.

According to George, Gracie never said anything about the affair until seven years later, when she was shopping with Jack Benny's wife, Mary. They were in the silver department at Saks Fifth Avenue when Gracie said to Mary, "You know, I wish George would cheat again. I really need a new centerpiece."

George's biographer, Martin Gottfried, speculated that Gracie and George didn't have much of a sex life, but he conceded no one really knew. George's memoirs avoid the subject, except to say that "Gracie and I had a wonderful life together, and a wonderful marriage, and sex was a part of it, but not the major part."

❧—❧

The major part of it was work. They mastered every medium they tried. In 1930, they signed a deal with Paramount to make movies, then in 1932 moved their act to radio. "The George Burns and Gracie Allen Show" was only a moderate success until 1933, when they came up with the gimmick of Gracie searching for her missing brother. She kept showing up as a guest on other shows, where she'd ask if anyone had seen him. Her brother, she explained, was the man who invented an umbrella with holes so you could see when the rain stopped.

The stunt brought Gracie's humor to a new audience and made the show a hit. The only one who wasn't happy about it was her real brother, George Allen, who got so fed up with reporters hounding him that he briefly disappeared for real.

In 1940, after their ratings had dipped a bit, George and Gracie introduced the radio audience to their two real-life children, both adopted. Their five-year-old son Ronnie became a regular character on the show, and the ratings bounced back.

In 1950, "The George Burns and Gracie Allen Show" made the jump to television, and again they were a hit. The characters remained basically the same, though George introduced the novel technique of sometimes stepping off the set to address the television audience directly. It was an unusual, almost modernist approach for early television, but it was a perfect fit for George's cynical, wisecracking style.

Gracie, however, was increasingly dissatisfied. She'd never loved show business as much as George. Starting in the early fifties, she suffered angina pains and, coupled with the migraine headaches she'd had for years, they made retirement very tempting.

Each year, when CBS renewed the show's contract, George had to coax Gracie to sign. In the fall of 1957, when he called to tell her they had yet another deal, she hung up on him. The next spring, Gracie had a heart attack and, though she recovered, there was now no question that this would be her final season. The last episode of "The George Burns and Gracie Allen Show" was filmed on June 4, 1958.

Gracie had no regrets about giving it up. When someone asked her if she missed the good old days, she scoffed. "Believe me, the really good days are right now. What was so good about running from train to train, living out of a suitcase, and having a quick bite if we had time?"

Not so for George. "Well, I sort of liked running from train to train," he said.

He tried to continue the series without Gracie, but "The George Burns Show" flopped. He tried to find another partner, working with Connie Stevens, Madeline Kahn, Bernadette Peters, Ann-Margret, and (most successfully) Carol Channing. But as Lou Weiss, the chairman of the board of the William Morris Agency and also George's nephew, said: "None of them was ever Gracie. Gracie was Gracie."

George had always joked that he was nothing but Gracie's straight man. "Gracie and I had no problems with our careers, because we only had one—hers," he said. "We made our entrance holding hands, and when we got to center stage, I said to Gracie, 'How's your brother?' and she spoke for thirty-eight years. And that's how I became a star." Another time he wrote: "The act was called Burns and Allen, but it should have been Gracie Allen and What's-His-Name."

George knew this wasn't true, of course. His reactions to Gracie on stage, not to mention his writing and production work behind the scenes, was crucial to their success. But there was no denying that Gracie's retirement and the failure of "The George Burns Show" brought back painful memories. "I'd been a failure until I'd met Gracie, and now I'd failed at the first thing I tried after she retired," he said.

Worse, Gracie's health was deteriorating. She suffered another heart attack in 1961, after which she was able to go out less and less. In 1964, Gracie suffered her final heart attack, and on August 27, at the age of fifty-eight, she died.

"For forty years my act consisted of one joke," George wrote. "And then she died."

❬•—•❭

At sixty-eight, there seemed nothing left for George. Certainly those who knew him best thought he would retire. "I believe George thought his career was over," said Paul Henning, one of the writers on the show. "We didn't know what in the world he would do."

Astoundingly, he was nowhere near done. He kept acting with various partners, and in 1975, when he was 79, he made a triumphant comeback as a retired vaudeville performer in Neil Simon's *The Sunshine Boys*. He won an Academy Award for best supporting actor.

Two years later, he played God in the hit movie *Oh, God*. In 1984, when at the age of 93 he starred in the second of its sequels, he said: "Why shouldn't I play God? Anything I do at my age is a miracle."

George died on March 9, 1996, at the age of 100—ending a show business career that lasted 93 years.

In his later years, George was often seen in the company of younger women. "People often ask me why I don't go out with women my own age," he explained. "I tell them the truth—there are no women my age."

But no one could interpret George's wisecracks—or his success after Gracie's death—as meaning that he'd in any way forgotten her. In 1989, he published *All My Friends*, one of a series of bestselling memoirs. In it, he wrote: "She was my wife, my lover, my partner in our act, and most important, my best friend. . . . I knew what Gracie looked like with her makeup off, and she knew what I looked like without my toupee. And she still loved me."

In his 1988 bestseller, *Gracie: A Love Story*, George wrote: "I still go to Forest Lawn Cemetery once a month to see her. I stand in front of her marble monument and tell her everything that's going on in my life.

"I don't know if she hears me," he added, "but I know that after speaking to her, I feel better."

Desi Arnaz
and Lucille Ball

*C*onsidering how they looked when they first met, it's remarkable either Lucille Ball or Desi Arnaz gave the other a second glance.

It was June 1940 on the movie set for *Too Many Girls*, a Rogers and Hart extravaganza about college football in which Desi was playing an Argentine player and Lucy a coed ingenue. Desi was wearing old clothes, having just filmed a football scene. Lucille had just come from the set of *Dance, Girl, Dance*, another movie in which she was appearing. She and her costar, Maureen O'Hara, had just filmed a fight scene, and Desi later recalled that Lucille looked like "a two-dollar whore who had been badly beaten by her pimp." She had a black eye, her hair was hanging down over her face, and her dress was coming apart at the seams.

But neither clothes nor makeup mattered.

"It was like Wow! A bolt of lightning! Lucille fell like a ton of bricks," O'Hara recalled. "They hit it off right away."

"It was not love at first sight," Lucille argued. "It took five minutes."

The two flirted on the set, with Desi offering to teach her to rumba, a dance she had to learn for the movie. She called him Dizzy, then Daisy. He called her Lucy, even though she'd always been known as Lucille.

"I never liked 'Lucille,'" he later explained. "That name had been used by other men. 'Lucy' was mine alone."

❧— ☙

No one expected the relationship to last.

Desi was a notorious womanizer. He'd already had a brief fling with Betty Grable, and he was engaged at the time he met Lucy. "No wonder they picked you for *Too Many Girls*," she screamed at him, after hearing rumors that he was going out with one of the chorus girls.

They were at very different stages of their careers. Lucy was twenty-nine, Desi twenty-three. She had achieved, not quite stardom, but at least a steady flow of starring roles in second-rate movies and secondary roles in bigger films. Desi's conga dance routine had been a hit in New York, but *Too Many Girls* was his first movie.

Their backgrounds were equally incompatible. She was from a small town in upstate New York; he was from Cuba. She had panhandled for subway fare so she could get to acting classes in New York. He had grown up with speedboats and racehorses, until Fulgencio Batista came to power in 1933 and stripped his family of its wealth.

Desi wasn't even her type. Until then, Lucy had gone out with older men, like producer Pandro Berman and director Al Hall. She wasn't the type to head for the "casting couch," but there was no denying these were the kind of men who could advance her career.

They were both jealous, both temperamental, both stubborn. The cast of *Too Many Girls* took bets on how long it would last. The winner was Eddie Bracken. "I had more faith in it than anyone," he recalled. "I said six months."

But none of this mattered. "I was terrified at what I was doing and wondered if I had chosen wisely," Lucy remembered. "Yet I sensed in Desi a great need. Beneath that dazzling charm was a homeless boy who had no one to care for him, worry about him. And I wanted him and only him as the father of my children."

Lucy and Desi were as much in love as any mismatched couple from one of the era's screwball comedies. Six months after they met, they decided to elope. Desi figured he had enough time to marry Lucy and get back for his band's late show at the Roxy Theater, but they were held up because he'd forgotten to buy a wedding ring. A quick stop at Woolworth's remedied that.

"It turned my finger green from the first time I wore it, but it signified so much to me that I never wanted to take it off," Lucy recalled.

Desi missed the early performances but made it back for the last show. The management, having been notified of the reason he was late, passed out packets of rice to the audience. As Desi and Lucy walked out onto the stage, they were engulfed in a blizzard of rice.

"Two sympathetic people of different temperaments and backgrounds fused in a union of opposites," wrote Kathleen Brady, Ball's most recent biographer. But she added, "In the movies love suffices for the debutante and the butler, but they have the advantage of a director who knows to yell cut before the real challenges begin."

⁂

The marriage, alas, did not change Desi's ways. With Lucy in Hollywood and Desi in New York, he was as promiscuous as ever. They would fight and make up and fight again, often by long-distance.

After one such fight, Lucy hung up the phone and went to bed, only to be awakened by the operator from Desi's hotel.

"Why haven't you called Desi back?" the operator asked, having apparently listened in on more than one of their fights. "He's in his room feeling miserable. He didn't mean any of the things he said, and I'm sure you didn't either."

Lucy broke up laughing and immediately called Desi back.

"The reason we survived this constant arguing, fighting, and accusation for so many years was because we had something extra-special going for us," Desi later said. "Our sexual relationship was heavenly. And perhaps even more important, we had a good sense of humor. We were able to laugh at ourselves and at our sometimes absurd and stupid arguments."

"In those early years, our fights were a kind of lovemaking," Lucy remembered. "Desi and I enjoyed them."

Indeed, the fighting was so much a part of their lives that the couple built a separate guest house so Desi wouldn't always have to go to a hotel. It also helped that Lucy was a lot quicker to blame Desi's lovers than Desi. Actress Janis Carter remembered Lucy's complaints: "She would say, 'That woman is blatant!'"

By 1944, however, the fighting and philandering had gotten to Lucy. Just before their fourth wedding anniversary, she filed for divorce. Then, the day before they were scheduled to appear in court, Desi invited Lucy to dinner. They ended up spending the night together.

The next morning, Lucy got up, kissed Desi on the cheek, and told him she'd be back as soon as she could. Desi recalled, "She'd bought a new suit and a new hat and she didn't want to disappoint all the reporters who would be down there at the courthouse."

The court granted Lucy a divorce. True to her word—and having taught Desi his lesson—Lucy then went right home to him, which by California law instantly invalidated the divorce.

Minus the sex, it might well have been an episode of "I Love Lucy."

It was radio, not television, that first made Lucy a star. In 1948, she was a moderately successful movie star, making good money and getting regular roles but nowhere near a household name. In fact, according to a poll RKO commissioned, only a third of moviegoers could identify her photo. Desi's future in

Hollywood seemed even bleaker: there weren't many roles for Latinos to start with, and most of the big ones were going to Ricardo Montalban.

Then came "My Favorite Husband."

The show first aired on CBS radio in July 1948. Lucy starred as Liz Cooper, a suburban housewife married to a banker played by Richard Denning. Gale Gordon, who later played Lucy's short-tempered banker boss on "Here's Lucy," played Denning's short-tempered banker boss. The show had much in common with "I Love Lucy"—minus Desi. And it was enough of a success that when CBS started turning their radio shows into TV shows, it was a logical choice.

For Lucy, however, a move to television involved some risk. Since movie studios rightly saw the new medium as a serious threat, they prohibited their stars from appearing without special permission. So a TV show could mean the end of Lucy's movie career.

But her movie career had still not catapulted her into the ranks of the top stars, and at age thirty-nine, time was running out. She figured she didn't have all that much to lose. And on the personal front, she had a lot to gain. If Desi could be her costar, that would get him off the road (and away from all the women he met there). It just might be the way to make their marriage work.

CBS was less taken with the idea of Desi replacing Richard Denning as Lucy's husband. Network executives argued that he was a bandleader, not an actor. Besides, as Desi later described the network's position, there was no way audiences would believe that an "All-American typical redhead" was married to a "Cuban Pete."

"What do you mean, nobody'll believe it?" Lucy retorted. "We *are* married."

To convince the network that audiences would accept their marriage, Lucy and Desi took their act on the road. They formed Desilu Productions (after rejecting other combinations like Arnaball, Ballarnaz, and Lucydes) and put together a series of slapstick routines in which Lucy played a movie star trying to join Desi's band.

The tour was a moderate success—enough to turn a profit for Desilu, but not enough to change minds at CBS. After all, this type of vaudeville act was even closer to extinction than radio and hardly proof that it would work on television.

So Lucy and Desi shot their own pilot, a variation of their vaudeville act. When NBC expressed interest in the show, CBS reconsidered. "I Love Lucy" was born.

The first episode aired in October 1951. By November, the show was such a hit that telephone companies reported a substantial drop in calls during its half-hour slot. In Chicago, Marshall Field's department store posted a sign in its window saying "We love Lucy, too, so we're closing on Monday nights."

Lucy was everywoman, and everyone loved her. Lucymania reached its peak in 1952 and 1953 when both the character Lucy

Ricardo and the real-life Lucille were pregnant. At first, the network was reluctant to show a pregnant woman, but they were even more afraid of antagonizing their stars.

In October 1952, Desilu filmed "Lucy is Enceinte." (The network inexplicably decided that the Spanish word for *pregnant* could be used on the air but not the English.) The episode was supposed to end with Ricky and Lucy singing joyfully, but the emotions surrounding the pregnancy were so strong—Lucy had had several miscarriages—that both stars started sobbing and couldn't finish the number.

"It was one of the most moving things I've ever seen," recalled Jess Oppenheimer, the show's producer. "The studio audience and the production crew cried right along with them."

Oppenheimer ordered a retake, but everybody yelled no. Oppenheimer went with the first take.

On January 19, 1953, CBS aired "Lucy Goes to the Hospital," in which Ricky, Fred, and Ethel grab a cab, almost forgetting, of course, to bring Lucy. That night, forty-four million Americans—more than one-fifth of the population—tuned in to see Lucy give birth to Ricky Ricardo Jr.

Remarkably, that was the same day the real-life Lucy also gave birth—to Desi Arnaz Jr. (Desi Jr. did not play Little Ricky on the show, because his parents didn't want his older sister, Lucie, to wonder why she wasn't also on television.)

❀•—•❀

For a moment, it seemed that Lucy and Desi would have as happy an ending as Lucy and Ricky. The baby was healthy; the show was a huge success; Desi was turning Desilu into a television powerhouse that would produce not just "I Love Lucy," but other hits such as "Our Miss Brooks" and "Make Room for Danny."

Even Senator Joseph McCarthy's House Un-American Activities Committee couldn't suppress the couple. In 1953, the committee investigated Lucy because she'd once registered to vote Communist. Lucy testified that she'd done so only to please her aging grandfather. This was true, but given the dangerous mood of the times, this innocuous admission might still have been damaging.

Not for Lucy, though. On September 11, after word of the investigation leaked to the press, Desi took the stage prior to the day's filming. Instead of the usual warm-up, he turned serious. "Lucy has never been a Communist. Not now, and never will be," he said. "I want you to meet my favorite wife—my favorite redhead—that's the only thing red about her, and even that's not legitimate—Lucille Ball!"

The audience gave Lucy a standing ovation. That night's episode, by chance, was "The Girls Go into Business," as capitalist a title as anyone could ask for. Public support for Lucy was so wholehearted that some historians see it as a turning point after which McCarthyism was never again so powerful a force in Hollywood.

But the couple's political problems were more easily solved than their personal ones. Though Lucy had hoped working together would keep Desi away from other women, it didn't work out that way. For Desi, the pressures of running Desilu, of acting and directing, perhaps even of seeing Lucy all day long intensified his need to escape into drunken revels, sometimes with other women.

In 1959, Lucy finally asked for a divorce. It's hard to pin her decision on one incident, but the breaking point may have come in September, when Desi was charged with being drunk in public. The arrest was all the more embarrassing because it took place on Vista Street, the site of numerous West Hollywood brothels.

"Anonymity is a great thing when you're unhappy," Lucy later wrote. "But when Desi made it public domain, I knew I couldn't be publicly embarrassed any longer."

In February 1960, just before Lucy formally filed for divorce—this time for keeps—Desi directed the last of the half-hour episodes of "I Love Lucy." Both Lucy and Desi realized it might be the last time they played Lucy and Ricky. At the end of the episode, the script called for them to kiss and make up, as usual. They kissed.

"This was not just an ordinary kiss for a scene in a show," Desi wrote. "It was a kiss that would wrap up twenty years of love and friendship, triumphs and failures, ecstasy and sex, jealousy and regrets, heartbreaks and laughter."

After the kiss, Lucy and Desi stood staring at each other. Then Lucy said, "You're the director. You're supposed to say 'cut.'"

"I know," Desi said. "Cut, goddam it!"

3

Katharine Hepburn and Spencer Tracy

*I*t's a cliché in Hollywood love stories that, when the leading man and the leading lady first meet, they detest each other. So it should come as no surprise that the couple whose movies proclaimed war—and love—between the sexes should have clashed instantly.

Katharine Hepburn met Spencer Tracy at the MGM studios in August 1941. They were about to begin work on their first movie together, *Woman of the Year*. Hepburn spotted Tracy walking with the producer, Joseph Mankiewicz.

Hepburn, who was about five feet nine inches tall and wearing heels, realized she was taller than the five-foot-ten Tracy.

"Mr. Tracy, I think you're a little short for me," she said.

"Don't worry," Mankiewicz answered. "He'll cut you down to size."

As Hepburn walked away, Tracy railed about her handshake (too firm) and her suit (unlike other stars of the era, Hepburn never wore a dress).

"Not me, boy," said Tracy. "I don't want to get messed up in anything like this."

In front of the camera, sparks continued to fly. The first scene they shot took place in a bar where the tough sportswriter (Tracy) and the famous columnist (Hepburn) tangled over her suggestion that baseball be banned during World War II. In the middle of the scene, Hepburn accidentally spilled a glass of water.

"Spencer handed me a handkerchief, and I took his handkerchief," she recalled. "I thought, 'Oh you old so-and-so, you're going to make me mop it up right in the middle of the scene.'"

Hepburn decided to embarrass Tracy right back by making a big show of cleaning up not just the table, but the floor.

"I mopped and mopped and [director] George Stevens kept the camera running," Hepburn continued. "Spencer just smiled."

The unscripted scene made it into the movie, and audiences loved it. They continued to love Hepburn and Tracy through eight more movies in which his cranky yet good-hearted hero and her accomplished yet sometimes overbearing heroine do battle and fall in love.

In 1949, they were husband-and-wife lawyers on opposite sides of a murder case in *Adam's Rib*. Three years later, in *Pat and Mike*, she was an elegant athlete and he her roguish manager. Their movie partnership did not end until Tracy's death in 1967, just after they finished shooting *Guess Who's Coming to Dinner*?

For the twenty-six years they were on-screen together, they were also a couple off-screen—in spite of the fact that he remained married to someone else. Even more astounding, though they spent much of their time in Hollywood, the gossip capital of the world, their true-life romance remained a secret until many years after his death. And when their story did become known, it turned out to be even more intriguing than any of their movies.

❧—❧

Misleading as a star's image can often be, for both Tracy and Hepburn, what they portrayed on-screen had a lot in common with who they were off-screen.

She *was* aristocratic, headstrong, independent. He *was* stubborn, gruff, rugged.

"They were not just different," noted Garson Kanin, who cowrote *Adam's Rib* and *Pat and Mike*. "They were two very different sorts of people—altogether separate breeds, worlds apart."

She grew up rich; he was middle-class. Her politics were left-wing; his were more middle-of-the road. She was intellectual; he was down-to-earth. He was Hollywood's number two star when they met in 1940, right behind Clark Gable, whom he would soon pass. Her career had been up and down: she had won an Oscar in 1933, but a string of failures had labeled her box-office poison before she rebounded with *The Philadelphia Story* in 1940.

They were bound to collide. She liked to rehearse a scene over and over; he liked to be more natural in front of the camera. (His advice to aspiring actors: "Learn your lines, and don't bump into the furniture.")

"Everybody was sort of on tenterhooks waiting to see who would blow first," Mankiewicz recalled.

It turned out to be a classic case of opposites attracting. "One day he was talking . . . about 'that woman' and the next he showed up calling her Kathy," Mankiewicz continued. "Everyone was immensely relieved."

In their movies, it was generally Spencer who came out ahead, though not, of course, without a struggle. *Woman of the Year* set the tone. Originally, the movie was to end at a baseball game, with Kate's character having become an even bigger fan than Spencer's. But the producer and director insisted on Kate learning a lesson about the importance of domesticity. The final scene, in its final version, has her in the kitchen, ineptly preparing her husband's breakfast. He then consoles her for making a mess.

Mankiewicz and Stevens, as well as the movie's audience, were pleased. Explained Mankiewicz: "Now women could turn to their schmuck husbands and say, 'She may know the president, but she can't even make a cup of coffee.'"

It was not just an exceedingly chauvinistic ending, but a repudiation, it seemed, of all that Katharine Hepburn stood for. A highly successful and independent woman had been put in her place.

The ending of *Adam's Rib* strikes a similar note. Kate's character, a defense attorney, gets her client off after she (the client) has killed her abusive husband. But her district-attorney husband (Spencer) teaches her a more important lesson. Pretending to be infuriated, he pulls a gun on her to demonstrate the danger of taking the law into your own hands. The gun turns out to be made of licorice, but Kate has learned her lesson. (Of the couple's comedies, only *Pat and Mike* lets Kate come out on top, when she gets to beat up a couple of hoods threatening him.)

That was Hollywood, at least in the forties and fifties. No one could reasonably expect popular movies to advance a feminist agenda. What was far more perplexing was that, in their off-screen relationship, Spencer seemed even more fully the boss.

There was never any question, for example, who would get top billing. On all their films, even as Kate matched his fame, Spencer's name came first. Kanin once suggested to him that, perhaps, it should be "ladies first."

"This is a movie, chowderhead," Spencer said, "not a lifeboat."

Spencer did not hesitate to put Kate in her place. Recalled Stanley Kramer, who directed three of his movies without her and one with her: "Kate would venture one of her strong opinions about Russian missiles, for example, and Spence would sneer at her, 'So that's another one of those subjects you know all about.' Instead of blowing her top, like she would with anyone else, Kate would just giggle and say, 'Oh, Spencuh,' just like that. And Spence would come back with . . . 'Why do you always talk like you've got a feather up your ass?'"

"She'd make a funny face at him," Kramer said, "but we got on with it. She'd take anything from him. She'd take nothing from anybody else."

This went way beyond banter. In 1942, guests at the Beverly Hills Hotel would regularly see Katharine Hepburn sleeping in the hallway outside Spencer Tracy's room. This meant he'd been drinking heavily, and he wouldn't let her in. But she stayed right outside in case he needed her help.

Why would a fiercely independent woman submit to this?

Some of those who knew them both were certain that, in spite of Spencer's apparently abusive behavior, he loved and respected her deeply.

Kramer: "When it came to important things . . . she *never* took a backseat." George Cukor, who directed *Adam's Rib* and *Pat and Mike*: "He could be extremely gruff with her, that was the little roughneck boy from Milwaukee filtering through, but he had enormous respect for her and he *listened* to her. . . . I'd discuss a suggested change with him on the set and he'd say, 'Let's see what Kate thinks.'"

Still, there was no question that Spencer came first. Some of Kate's more psychologically oriented biographers trace her acquiescence back to the age of thirteen, when her brother committed suicide at an aunt's home and Kate opened the door to his room and discovered his body. Wrote Barbara Leaming: "In

1921, she had failed to sense the danger when her brother . . . locked himself in a room at Aunty Towle's; Kate would never make that mistake again."

So she positioned herself outside another door behind which there was another troubled man, this time determined to make sure he would do himself no harm.

Kate's own explanation for her behavior, in her 1991 memoir, was much simpler: love meant sacrifice. "This was not easy for me because I was definitely a *me me me* person," she explained. "He didn't like this or that. I changed this and that . . . Food— we ate what he liked. We did what he liked. We lived a life which he liked.

"I wanted him to be happy—safe—comfortable. I liked to wait on him—listen to him—feed him—talk to him—work for him. . . . I struggled to change all the qualities which I felt he didn't like. Some of them which I thought were my best I thought he found irksome. I removed them, squelched them as far as I was able.

"I loved Spencer Tracy," she wrote. "He and his interests and his demands came first."

Petruchio could have asked nothing more of his own Kate.

Though they stayed together until his death, Kate and Spencer never married; indeed, he never divorced his first wife, Louise.

Some biographers have attributed this to Spencer and Louise being Catholic, but there was more to it than that. They had two children, one of whom was deaf. Louise founded and served as president of the John Tracy Clinic (named for their son), an organization dedicated to helping deaf children. For Louise, the marriage to Spencer was undeniably helpful in the organization's Hollywood fund-raising. And for Spencer, his son's deafness added to his guilt about his relationship with Kate, making it all the more difficult to leave Louise.

Kate never pushed the issue, perhaps because—in spite of her love for Spencer—she recognized that she needed some time away from him. "I have always thought that marriage was a funny sort of institution," she explained. "Sometimes I wonder if men and women really suit each other at all. It's inevitable that they should come together now and again, but how well suited are they to living in the same house? Perhaps they should live next door and visit every now and then."

So that is how they lived their lives. Kate spent quite a bit of time away from Spencer, for example, when she performed on Broadway or traveled to Africa for the filming of *The African Queen*, while he remained in Hollywood. But she always returned to him, especially when she was worried that he was drinking too much.

When Spencer needed her, he always came first. If he was sick, she would quit work to be with him, and during the last six or seven years of his life, she moved in next door to keep a closer eye on his health.

That they never actually lived together, let alone married, helped keep their relationship a secret. Friends knew about it, of course, but they kept it to themselves. Even those in the press who suspected an affair restrained themselves, partly out of respect for Louise Tracy's work with the deaf, partly out of respect for Spencer and Kate. Their on-screen relationship seemed to consist of a lot more banter than sex, so the public was willing to believe that they were, as the MGM press releases always insisted, "staunch friends."

Occasionally, Kate and Spencer feared the secret might leak. In 1954, while he was staying at Claridge's in London (and she at the nearby Connaught), the management asked to speak to him about her daily visits. Spencer feared they were going to object to an affair on their premises, or worse, threaten to reveal it to the press. But it turned out that the management objected to Kate ignoring the hotel's dress code: she always wore pants in the lobby.

Kate, who would change for Spencer but not for others, claimed she didn't own a dress. She continued her daily visits to the hotel, but from then on she rode up to Spencer's suite in the freight elevator.

↪•—•⇀

In the early sixties, a few stories hinted that there might be more to the relationship than could be seen on the screen, but the secret remained intact even after Spencer's heart attack in 1967. Kate was the first on the scene; she heard him fall in the kitchen and rushed to his side to find him dead. But, out of respect for Louise, she did not attend his funeral.

A few days later, she called Louise and suggested they become friends. "Well, yes, but you see," Louise replied, "I thought you were only a rumor."

Kate did nothing to turn the rumor into a fact. Only after Louise's death in 1983 did Kate speak openly of her love for Spencer. And only then did she begin to wonder whether, perhaps, she and Spencer ought not to have made their love public. "It certainly would have been more simple," she wrote. "And actually it might have removed Spence's sense of guilt. It would have been honest."

But for that to happen, Kate continued, Louise would have had to have agreed to a divorce. "It would, I believe, have been ennobling to her. And supremely honest. And it would have made it easy for him to do . . . if he had felt that it was her idea, his guilt would have been removed.

Kate concluded: "If she'd done that she would have had to have been a saint. . . . Too much to ask, I agree." Kate could not ask Louise to make such a sacrifice.

Instead, she made it herself.

4

Dale Evans and
Roy Rogers

*F*or twenty years, they reigned as the King of the Cowboys and the Queen of the West. As the chroniclers
of popular culture Jane and Michael Stern wrote in
the book *Happy Trails*: "He shot the straightest and rode the
fastest and yodeled the sweetest and strummed hypnotic sage-
brush tunes about tumbling tumbleweeds on his guitar." And
she "was just about the prettiest cowgirl there ever was."

During the forties, the heyday of the B western, more than
eighty million people flocked to their movies each year. In the
fifties, the couple moved to television, and it seemed every kid
in America tuned in to see Roy and Dale. Or to tell the truth,
Roy and his horse, Trigger—and then perhaps Dale.

The show began with a shot of Roy on Trigger, with the rest
of the cast racing behind them. The announcer introduced—
always in the same order—"Roy Rogers, King of the Cowboys,
Trigger, his golden palomino, and Dale Evans, Queen of the
West." Dale could find some comfort in knowing that at least
she came before "Pat Brady, their comical sidekick, and Roy's
wonder dog, Bullet."

On-screen, Roy always got the bad guys. If, in the process,
he also got the girl, well, that was okay but clearly not his top
priority. In 1943, *Life* magazine put it this way: "He always wins
the girl though he doesn't kiss her. He kisses his horse." Or as
Roy explained, "We had to watch ourselves. If we got too

romantic onscreen, we knew we would hear from those boys out there who were allergic to 'mushy stuff.'"

Off-screen, though, things did get a bit mushy.

Roy and Dale followed very different trails to Hollywood. For Roy's family—impoverished farmers in Ohio—it was not Hollywood that beckoned, but the California of John Steinbeck's *Grapes of Wrath*. In 1930, like so many others during the Depression, they piled their belongings into a beat-up van and headed west in search of work. In California, they joined an army of migrant workers, moving from harvest to harvest. (Roy saw Steinbeck at one of the workers' camps, though they didn't speak.)

Sometimes Roy took time off to sing with a group known as the Sons of the Pioneers, but their pay—if any—was often just their supper. In New Mexico, one such gratefully accepted meal came from Arlene Wilcox. Arlene and Roy kept exchanging letters, and in June 1936, they married. The couple adopted a baby girl, then Arlene gave birth to a daughter.

The Sons of the Pioneers gradually started earning money instead of food, and then began getting bit parts in the "singing cowboy" movies that were then popular. Roy's big break came in 1938 when Gene Autry, the most popular of the cowboys, walked out of Republic Studios because of a contract dispute.

The studio, eager to put Autry in his place, offered Autry's starring role in *Under Western Stars* to Roy. Like most of Republic's movies, it was definitely a B western, but back then B westerns had a large and loyal following, and Roy was soon a star. Between 1936 and 1942, he made thirty-six movies, each about an hour long.

He played Billy the Kid, Wild Bill Hickok, Buffalo Bill, and other parts—even bad guys—before it became clear that audiences loved him best as Roy Rogers. The formula was pretty simple. "I sang about a half-dozen songs in each picture, and even though I started out thinking of myself as more a singer than an actor, I eventually learned acting," Roy recalled. "If I was a bad guy, I didn't smile; if I was a good guy, I had plenty of pleasant personality and a lot of smiles."

Trigger was with Roy from the start, and he soon was getting second billing as The Smartest Horse in the Movies. Before Dale came along, Roy was teamed with various actresses, most often Mary Hart. "We never kissed or anything," Roy said of Mary, "but she balanced all the action with a nice, soft touch and gave the movie someone I could sing to."

Unlike Roy, Dale set off for California with Hollywood very much her goal. She worked her way up as a singer and dancer, first in Memphis and then in Louisville, Dallas, and Chicago, before making her way west. She was married twice and had a child when she was just fifteen, but she pretended her son was her brother so producers wouldn't think she was too old.

For a while, Roy and Dale shared the same agent—Art Rush—but Dale dropped Rush because she felt he was spending too much time on Roy's career and not enough on hers. "I told Mr. Rush I was fed up with him and his singing cowboy," Dale recalled. "I intended to find myself an agent who put me and my career first."

It was certainly ironic, then, when in 1944 Republic asked her to play opposite Roy in *The Cowboy and the Senorita*. "I never had thought of myself doing a Western," Dale said. "Sure, I had liked cowboy pictures as a child, but that was as a child. As a professional actor, my goals were grander than that. I thought I wanted to be in a sophisticated musical comedy— something debonair, urbane, and adult."

Still, Dale was ambitious and she took the part. One problem that immediately surfaced was that, though she grew up in Texas, she hadn't been on a horse since she was seven years old.

In one scene, when she was supposed to come cantering down a hill after Roy and Trigger, Dale bounced so hard that her caps (which she had bought to advance her career) flew out of her mouth.

"When I finally managed to stop the horse, Roy came over and said, 'I never saw so much sky between a woman and a horse in all my born days,'" Dale said. Roy suggested riding lessons, and he began to instruct Dale himself.

During another scene, Dale's horse bolted, leaving Dale clinging to the horse's side. Roy raced after her and pulled Dale onto Trigger just as she was about to slide off her horse.

"For me, no movie scene could have been so breathtaking," Dale remembered. "And no make-believe cowboy was ever as heroic as Roy Rogers appeared to me at that moment."

Roy too was clearly attracted to Dale. "She was a person who always looked like she had just stepped out of the shower—real fresh and clean; and she was a good sport too," he said.

But Roy was, as that 1943 *Life* article put it, "purity rampant." And though Dale had divorced her second husband, Roy remained married and faithful to Arlene.

Then, in November 1946, eight days after giving birth to their third child and first son, Arlene died suddenly from a massive brain embolism. After that, Dale and Roy became even closer, though at first they remained just friends.

Roy, after all, was grieving, and Dale, for her part, was still dreaming of starring alongside someone other than a cowboy and his horse. At one point in 1946, sick of being a sidekick, she quit Republic. But her singing career fizzled, and Dale quickly returned. "I would like to ride the range again," she told the studio bosses.

So Roy and Dale were together again—not just on-screen, but at rodeos, state fairs, auto races, and other events across the country. The nonstop schedule meant they spent most of the day with each other.

They started having dinner together on the road, though they certainly wouldn't have called it dating. "It was just two tired friends—people who work together—enjoying each other's company, sharing thoughts and feelings," said Dale.

Gradually, friendship turned to love. The couple came to know not just each other, but their children. In the fall of 1947, while they were waiting to be introduced at a rodeo in Chicago, Roy proposed. Naturally, they were on horseback. Roy was on Trigger, Dale on her horse Buttermilk.

Right after Roy slipped the ring on her finger, Trigger bounded out of the chute. When Buttermilk caught up to him, Dale accepted. They were married that New Year's Eve.

❦

In August 1950, Dale gave birth to a daughter, Robin Elizabeth Rogers.

"When I learned I was pregnant, Roy wanted a boy and I wanted a girl," Dale said. "But neither of us was fussy. We were thrilled to be having a baby of either sex—just so long as he or she was healthy."

She wasn't. Dale had contracted German measles during her pregnancy, and the child suffered from Down's syndrome as well as a defective heart. Doctors recommended that Roy and Dale institutionalize Robin. So did the studio, which didn't like the idea of their stars being seen with anything other than a perfect child.

Dale recalled the couple's agony. "Why did this happen to us? The question haunted me," she said. "I thought Robin's affliction might be punishment for my sins—for my pride, my ambition, my failures as a mother."

Increasingly, Dale turned to religion to sustain her. "Had I not been a Christian, it would have just killed me," she later said.

Dale and Roy rearranged their lives so they could raise Robin. The child was better able to breathe away from the smog of Hollywood Hills, so they moved to the San Fernando Valley.

Roy's three children by Arlene, who had at first resented their stepmother, now pitched in to help with the baby. Said Dale: "I hardly realized it at the time, but Robin's presence was helping us grow close as a family."

The family planned a special celebration for Robin's second birthday, and they filled her room with new toys. But two days before her birthday, Robin's heart gave out and she died.

Dale wrote Robin's story and called it *Angel Unaware*. The book, which became a Christian bestseller, concluded with Robin asking: "And now, Father, please . . . could I just go out and try my wings?"

Robin's life also inspired Dale to write a song. "Roy had a cute theme song at the time called 'Smiles Are Made Out of the Sunshine,'" she said. "It was popular, but I felt it wasn't Western enough, and it didn't say enough about what it means to be a cowboy—especially when the trails you ride *aren't* always sunny ones."

So she wrote what became one of television's favorite themes: "Some trails are happy ones, others are blue/It's the way you ride the trail that counts/Here's a happy one for you/Happy trails to you until we meet again/Happy trails to you, keep smilin' until then."

Two months after Robin died, Dale and Roy returned home with two newly adopted children, and they went on to adopt two more children after that. The family later suffered two more tragedies: Debbie, the Korean orphan they'd adopted, was killed in a bus accident, and Sandy, an abused child they'd taken in, died in the armed services.

But their surviving children remember mostly happy, if often chaotic, childhoods. Said Roy Jr.: "My parents, even though they were busy, even though they were loved by millions, they gave me the time and attention I needed."

Dale generally handled the pressures of acting and raising all the kids without losing her temper. But she remembered one time when Roy Jr. and Sandy were wrestling in the living room, screaming, knocking over things, and ignoring their mother's pleas to stop. "I walked away, got out my stage pistol, loaded it with blanks, and fired it into the air six times," she said. "Those were the loudest explosions those boys had ever heard indoors. They were frozen in their tracks.

"And for a precious short while," she added, "they were quiet."

❧—❧

In 1951, after more than eighty movies, Roy and Dale moved their act to television. "The Roy Rogers Show" ran until 1957, and was followed by "The Roy Rogers and Dale Evans Show" in 1962 and 1963.

Television made them more popular than ever, especially among kids. "Their West," wrote Jane and Michael Stern, "was a magical American landscape full of promise and hope in which goodness was always rewarded and bad guys always got what they deserved."

This was a West, of course, that existed only in Hollywood. But, shocking as it may seem in these more cynical times, it was a West whose values Roy and Dale wholeheartedly embraced and by which they tried to live their lives.

Said Denver Pyle, an actor who worked with them: "They just went in front of the camera and were themselves. And fortunately they were the kind of people in their private life and in their social life that was the stuff that heroes are made of."

As a girl, Dale had dreamed of marrying Tom Mix, one of the earliest of the movie cowboys. "As things turned out," she said, "that crazy South Texas dream about my handsome cowboy hero and all those kids we'd raise and the happy trails we would ride together really did come true."

Roy died in 1988, Dale in 2001. Trigger died in 1965, but Roy had him mounted and he can still be seen at a museum now run by Roy Jr.

When Roy decided to preserve Trigger, Dale objected. Recalled Roy: "Dale howled at the thought of mounting Trigger, saying he deserved a nice funeral, but I reminded her he was my horse. 'Okay, but when you die, I'm going to put you on him!' she threatened.

"I told her that was fine with me, just so long as she made sure I was smiling."

5

Lauren Bacall and Humphrey Bogart

*W*arner Brothers' 1944 movie *To Have and Have Not* was based loosely on Ernest Hemingway's novel by that name. The studio, however, was much more excited by the similarities to its 1942 hit *Casablanca*, with Humphrey Bogart and Ingrid Bergman.

Like *Casablanca*, *To Have and Have Not* stars Humphrey Bogart as an American expatriate in French territory, this time named Harry and living on the West Indies island of Martinique. As with Rick in *Casablanca*, Harry finds a woman who jars him out of his cynicism and isolation, and who turns him into a hero of the Resistance.

Director Howard Hawks's seemingly impossible task was to find a woman who could do for the new movie what Ingrid Bergman had done for the earlier one. His wife, leafing through the latest issue of *Harper's Bazaar*, suggested the model on the cover. Within days, Betty Bacall (who took the screen name Lauren but continued to be known as Betty to her friends) was on her way to Hollywood.

Bacall seemed an unlikely candidate for the part of Slim, a sophisticated and wisecracking woman. Just nineteen and still a virgin, the actress had never been away from home except for summer camp. "It was pretty funny, my playing this woman of the world, this know-it-all, experienced sex-pot," she later wrote.

But Hawks must have seen something in the magazine and then in the screen test. "Watch yourself," Hawks told Bogie, "because you're supposed to be the most insolent man on the screen and I'm going to make a girl a little more insolent than you."

Bacall quickly proved the director's instincts were right, creating what became known as The Look. She would put her head down and raise her eyes, looking sultry. Later, she explained she'd done so just to stop from shaking, but it worked. It was especially sexy in the movie's most famous scene, shot in March, when she kisses the still-passive "Steve," as she called him.

"It's even better when you help," she says to Harry in her husky voice. "You don't have to say anything and you don't have to do anything. Not a thing. Oh, maybe just whistle. You know how to whistle, don't you, Steve? You just put your lips together and blow."

Harry couldn't resist Slim, nor Bogie Bacall.

So convincing were their love scenes that Hawks had to rewrite the script, which originally had Harry attracted to someone other than Slim. Remembered Bacall: "Halfway into the film Howard ran some of our scenes, showed them to Bogie, and with Bogie's help had come to the conclusion that no audience would believe anyone or anything could come between Slim and Steve. So scenes were adjusted accordingly."

"You can't beat chemistry," she added.

⤜•—•⤞

Few thought the romance would last, since Bogie was on his third marriage at the time. "He cried at every one of his weddings," Bacall later said. "And with good reason."

His latest marriage—to actress Mayo Methot—was in its sixth year and was indeed a cause for tears. Methot was as tough in person as Bogie was on the screen. They were so openly belligerent that they were known in Hollywood as the Battling Bogarts.

Earlier in the marriage, the noisy quarrels had often been followed by passionate reconciliations. Bogie and Methot seemed like characters from some screwball romance. "I wouldn't give you two cents for a dame without a temper," he said in *High Sierra*, and it seemed to apply to his life.

But as time passed, the fights weren't so funny. Methot became increasingly frustrated by the fact that her career was going nowhere while Bogie's soared. She drank more heavily and became increasingly violent, regularly throwing glasses at Bogie and at one point trying to stab him with a broken bottle.

By the time Bacall came along, there was little love left between Bogie and Methot. But he was still married, and given Methot's reputation for jealous rages, he was not eager to begin a confrontation.

So Bogie and Bacall's relationship, though known to the cast and crew, remained a secret from his wife. Once Bacall had to hide in his boat's bathroom when Methot made a surprise visit. When his wife called the studio, she was always told that he was out with the cast. On the set, people began to refer jokingly to Bacall as "the cast."

Hawks tried in vain to convince his protégée that her relationship with Bogie was doomed. "Bogie likes his life—he likes the drinking and he likes his wife," he told Bacall. "You're throwing away a whole career because of something that's just not going to happen. You're a damn fool."

Another time Hawks tried to divert the romance by setting up Bacall and Clark Gable, but that didn't work either. "He *was* dazzling to look at, but he stirred me not a bit," Bacall said.

As if to prove Hawks's point, when they wrapped up the shooting for *To Have and Have Not*, Bogie went home to Methot. Said Bacall: "Howard's voice saying 'Cut-print' brought the most memorable and important eleven weeks of my life to a close. Bogie said goodbye to everyone. . . . But the emptiness when he left! I felt as though everything that had given me care and support was being taken away. When would I see him—when would he call?"

A week later, she received a letter from Bogie: "I wish with all my heart that things were different. . . . And now I know what was meant by 'To say goodbye is to die a little'—because when I walked away from you that last time and saw you standing there so darling I did die a little in my heart."

In June, he wrote: "Darling, sometimes I get so unhappy because I feel that I'm not being fair to you . . . It's tragic that everything couldn't be all clean and just right for us instead of the way it is because we'd have so much fun together."

These were not the words of a man afraid to confront his wife or to commit to his lover. This was a man torn between his love for Bacall and his responsibility for Methot, now in the depths of her alcoholism. Perhaps too the age difference between the two gave him pause: Bogie was twenty-five years older.

So Bogie wavered and Bacall waited. In October 1944, he reunited with Bacall on the set of their next movie, *The Big Sleep*. That month, he left Methot, only to return two weeks later. In December, Bogie again moved out, then returned to Methot for Christmas.

But Christmas was a disaster, and Bogie was now finally convinced that he could not help his wife. He returned to Bacall, this time for good. For Christmas, he gave her a gold whistle. The inscription read: "If you want anything, just whistle."

Bacall and Bogie were married in May 1945, just eleven days after his divorce from Methot was finalized. It seemed that now, as a popular song about them went, they had it all. After three unhappy marriages, Bogie had met his match.

"She's wonderful," he said. "Startles me sometimes. I blink, and realize that she is looking at things with younger, clearer eyes and that she knows more than I do. And I say, 'Look here, how does she know more'n me?'—and I realize why. She's smarter'n me, that's all."

For Bacall, her marriage and career had all come together with remarkable speed. By the age of twenty-one, she had married a famous star and herself starred in two major hits.

The career success, she quickly learned, could not be sustained. There was nowhere to go but down, and after *To Have and Have Not* and *The Big Sleep*, her next movies were big disappointments. The critics were harsh. About *Confidential Agent*, the *Hollywood Review* wrote, "confidentially, it stinks." The magazine compared Bacall's performance to "a phonograph record that has become stuck on a turntable." Even Howard Hawks, who had discovered her, now noted her limitations. "She was not an actress," Hawks said. "She was a personality."

Bogie tried to cheer her up by making jokes about the reviews. "She was badly hurt," he said. But "pretty soon we got to the point where she was kidding about it too."

Bacall was attacked for her politics, as was Bogie. In 1947, the two were the most prominent members of a delegation from Hollywood that went to Washington to protest the actions of the House Un-American Activities Committee. When they were labeled Communists, Bogie backed away from his earlier position. As a result, he ended up antagonizing people on both sides of the issue.

What helped Bacall through these setbacks was that, in spite of the screen image Hawks had created of a woman more insolent than Bogie, her actual ambitions were more traditional. She wanted to be a wife and mother, and she was soon both. In 1949, she gave birth to Stephen (named after Bogie's character in *To Have and Have Not*), and three years later to Leslie.

Bogie's feelings about parenthood were more mixed. He was forty-nine when Stephen was born, and he was not so sure he wanted his wife's attentions diverted from him.

Bogie eventually got used to the idea, partly because it became clear that Bacall would put his needs first. In 1951, when Bogie went to Africa to film *The African Queen*, he assumed Bacall would come with him. "I hate like the devil to take Betty away from our son for such a long time," Bogie said in an interview. "The kid's only two and we're going to be away at least six months. But I can't see it any other way. My other marriages broke up on account of separations. Betty and I, we've been married six years, and I want to go on. So wherever I go, she goes."

Betty dutifully went to Africa, leaving Stephen with her mother. "I have a pain in my solar plexus when I remember how it felt to leave Steve behind," she recalled. "You suddenly say to yourself, 'Why the hell am I going—what am I doing?' Then, of course, you *know* what you're doing—you're going with your husband, who believes in no separations in marriage, who is working. Your life with him cannot stop for your son."

"So," she continued, "the heart tugs—the gut aches."

✦•— •✦

Bacall's devotion to Bogie was tested again in 1956, when he was diagnosed with cancer. She nursed him until his death a year later, and because the medical wisdom then was that a patient should not be told his illness was fatal, she had to live with the secret. Bogie was gallant in his final role, entertaining friends like Katharine Hepburn and Spencer Tracy even after painful radiation treatments.

During the last months of Bogie's life, Bacall became very close to Frank Sinatra, but she remained faithful to Bogie. "Having lived the better part of a year in the atmosphere of illness, I guess I not only began to depend on his presence . . . but looked forward to him," she later admitted. "He represented physical health—vitality. I needed that."

After Bogie's death, Bacall wanted to marry Sinatra, but that scared him off. "I could never play hard to get. I had been married to a grown-up," she said.

Bacall also admitted to earlier flirtations with Adlai Stevenson and Leonard Bernstein, but again there was no evidence that these ever led her to be unfaithful to Bogie.

"That's where the twenty-five-year difference in our ages showed," she later wrote. "He had the patience and trust in me to let me grow. He knew I was an innocent, never having had the chance to spread my sexual wings, so he allowed me my intermittent crushes.

"He had taught me early that all through one's life one meets people whom one is attracted to—sure, it's fun, but that's when you decide whether one weekend is worth it," she continued. "He valued character more than anything, and he trusted mine—I knew that and it kept me in check."

In 1961, Bacall married Jason Robards, but Bogie never receded from her thoughts. In fact, when Bacall and Robards divorced in 1969, he said bitterly, "I am tired of being Mrs. Bogart's second husband."

Bacall then went on to perform in a number of hit Broadway musicals, including *Applause*, for which she won a Tony Award, and *Woman of the Year*. For the first time since *The Big Sleep*, she was again a star.

Who deserved the credit for her comeback? "At the age of twenty I had grabbed at the sky and had touched some stars," she wrote. "And who but a twenty-year-old would think you could keep it? When it all went . . . why did I keep going?"

Her answer: "Bogie, with his great ability to love, never suppressing me, helping me to keep my values straight in a town where there were few, forcing my standards higher . . ."

6

Ossie Davis and Ruby Dee

*A*fter more than fifty years of marriage—a notable achievement in the world of show business—Ossie Davis and Ruby Dee are often asked their secret. Entertainers to the core, they sometimes respond with a joke. "God grabs my arm every time I get ready to swing the ax as he lies sleeping after a hard day of aggravating my very soul," Dee says. "That way I feel lucky not to be on death row, and I cross myself, hug him, and go for marriage one more day."

Davis tells how he decided to marry Dee. In 1947, when they were both struggling actors, he lent her $3,000 to invest in a black filmmaking project she was excited about. It was all the money he had.

"Three weeks later, Ruby told me a story that broke both her heart and mine," Ossie recalls. "The money she had borrowed was gone beyond all hope of retrieval, and she herself was broke. She softly said she was sorry, then started toward the door."

Ossie called her back, and they got to talking and ultimately to marriage. Ossie concludes: "A man is duty-bound to protect his investment."

Ossie's story is more than a joke. It gets to the heart of what brought them together and kept them together: their commitment to what they call "the struggle." Their joint investment in black filmmaking—at a time when that was politically and financially risky—was just the first foray in a lifetime of fighting for human and civil rights.

It was Ossie who emceed the 1963 March on Washington, where Martin Luther King Jr. gave his "I Have a Dream" speech. And it was Ossie who gave the eulogy at Malcolm X's funeral.

It was Ruby who starred in the groundbreaking 1961 movie *A Raisin in the Sun* and who Alex Haley called the "godmother" of his television series, *Roots*. And it was Ruby who worked quietly behind the scenes with such civil rights leaders as King, Malcolm, Whitney Young, Roy Wilkins, and A. Philip Randolph.

Said filmmaker Trey Ellis: "If there was a 'committee to defend' (be it the Rosenbergs, the Black Panthers, or Angela Davis), they were on the letterhead; if there was a rally to oppose (the Vietnam War, nuclear testing, apartheid in South Africa), they were on the podium. . . . It was all part of the struggle."

"We were joined together by the struggle," Ruby said. "Racism in America demands love." They were, both said, "in this thing together."

Though they remain active—and activist—they've also made plans for their death. "A special urn, large enough and comfortable enough to hold both our ashes," Ruby said. "Whoever goes first will wait inside for the other. When we are reunited at last, we want the family to say goodbye and seal the urn forever.

"Then on the side, in letters not too bold—but not too modest either—we want the following inscription: Ruby and Ossie—in this thing together."

Ossie and Ruby first met in 1945 during rehearsals for *Jeb*, a play about a black soldier returning from the Pacific to his native Louisiana, where he faces the Ku Klux Klan. Ossie was playing the title character, Ruby his girlfriend Libby. In one scene, Jeb defends himself against a false accusation by calling out, "You know me, you know Libby!"

Recalled Ruby: "My heart leaped when I heard him say instead, 'You know me, you know Ruby!'"

The relationship did not have much of a chance to develop, since *Jeb* closed after just nine performances. But they got another chance when both signed on to star in a national tour of *Anna Lucasta*, a Broadway hit.

"Thrown together, under all kinds of conditions, for more than nine months, it became a chance to rehearse our coming married life," said Ossie. By Christmas Eve 1946, after they sang carols and danced at a restaurant in St. Paul, Minnesota, he was head over heels in love.

Ossie hesitated about marriage, partly because Ruby was a divorcée and he'd been brought up in a household where divorce was tantamount to adultery. But he eventually bit the bullet and told her they might as well get married.

"Don't do me no favors," she responded. But she too was in love, and in December 1948, at a small ceremony in New Jersey, they were married.

Neither Broadway nor Hollywood was knocking on the newlyweds' door, especially since both were outspokenly leftist in the age of the blacklist. Ossie and Ruby survived by creating what he called "a kind of people's theater." They played in community centers, churches, synagogues, anyplace they could convert to a stage. Their biggest success of the period was *The World of Sholom Aleichem*, which they put on at various synagogues and in a hotel. "Two notebooks, two music stands or podiums, and our passion for great literature are all that was required," Ossie said.

During this period, Ossie wrote as well as acted in plays. His first play to be produced was *Alice in Wonder*, about a popular black entertainer pressured to testify against another black artist accused of being a Communist. Ruby played the entertainer's wife, who leaves him when he bows to the pressure.

Playing mostly to black audiences, the couple managed to get by. Said Ossie: "They were, and still are, the audience that never made us rich, but never let us down."

❖━━❖

The breakthrough to a wider public came in 1959 when Ruby starred alongside Sidney Poitier in Lorraine Hansbury's Broadway hit *A Raisin in the Sun*. Later that same year, Ossie took over for Poitier.

Stardom did not diminish Ruby and Ossie's focus on the political ramifications of what they were doing. The show's title came from Langston Hughes's poem, in which he asks: "What happens to a dream deferred?/Does it dry up/Like a raisin in the sun?" Or, Hughes wonders in the final line, "Does it explode?"

Ossie and Ruby worried that the warning of the poem and the play—that black frustration was on the verge of exploding—had been subverted by the Broadway production. The main character is Walter Lee Younger, whose dreams of better things have been long deferred.

"Sure, Walter, goaded by dreams of what he could not have in America because of racism, was about to explode, but not to worry," Ossie thought. "Lena, his mother, the strong and domineering head of the household, was totally in charge. America could depend on her to keep Walter under control, no matter what. The people who filled the theater night after night had nothing to worry about."

Still, even if the production was less revolutionary than its actors or playwright might have hoped, there was no question that, at the very least, it made white audiences think about racism. And it opened up opportunities for Ossie and Ruby they would otherwise never have had.

For Ossie, it meant he could finish and see produced his own play, *Purlie Victorious*, which he'd been working on for years. The play was inspired by an incident from Ossie's childhood in rural Georgia. When he was about six or seven years old, two white policeman picked him up for no reason, took him to the station house, and poured a jar of cane syrup over his head. As they laughed, so did Ossie: this was, he later realized, "the process of niggerization."

In *Purlie Victorious*, Purlie, played by Ossie, returns to his hometown with a convoluted plan to win back an inheritance that a white landlord had swindled from a black sharecropper. Purlie's girlfriend, played by Ruby, is supposed to pose as the woman inheriting the money. But at the crucial moment, she forgets her part and the plan goes hilariously awry. In the end, it all comes out okay.

The show was a hit, but again Ossie and Ruby worried whether its message was the right one. Purlie was more a traditional trickster than a sixties revolutionary; the characters, black and white, were more like the fools in *The World of Sholom Aleichem* than black militants or white racists. When she first read the play, Ruby compared it to a minstrel show.

"Ruby had a point," Ossie later wrote. "Black folk were determined to . . . put folk humor aside and put on war paint. . . . Was *Purlie Victorious*, with all its laughter, its gags, its schtick and one-liners, an act of betrayal?" He had started out writing a play about revenge and had ended up with everyone laughing—just as they all did when the cops poured syrup on his head.

But Ossie became convinced that laughter could be a weapon of change. Among those who told him so were W. E. B. DuBois, who came opening night, and Martin Luther King, who saw the one-hundredth performance. Malcolm X also liked the show, telling Ossie he thought that blacks laughing at whites was itself a revolutionary idea.

The sixties, of course, were a time of sexual as well as political revolution, and Ossie and Ruby were very much caught up in that as well. "It occurred to us . . . that extramarital sex was not what really destroyed marriages, but rather the lies and deception that invariably accompanied it—that was the culprit," Ossie explained. "So we decided to give ourselves permission to sleep with other partners if we wished—as long as what we did was honest as well as private, and that neither of us exposed the family to scandal or disease."

Ruby's recollection was a little different. "He says it was my idea that we should free each other from the vows of 'keep you only unto him/her as long as you both shall live.' Maybe it was. I only remember being determined not to be the fence blocking his view of the greener-looking grass on the other side."

Whoever thought of it first, both agreed to give it a try. Ruby had a brief affair with a classical musician; Ossie flirted openly with other actresses. But Ruby was quickly unhappy with the experiment. "It seemed . . . like a role in a play I could be rehearsing—the other woman, heifer, hussy, adventurer," Ruby remembered. "It really didn't seem like me at all . . . Somebody else was walking around in my skin.

"I knew that whatever adultery was, it wasn't freedom," she continued. "I need somebody to laugh with, to share values and life commitments, and to grow old together with. I need Ossie, for God's sake."

Ossie conceded the open marriage wasn't working, though he saw some value in it. "We turned each other loose and set great wheels in motion once again," he said. "I found myself having to compete with other men for my own wife's affection. It was a humbling, but also a stimulating experience. I'm glad we did it, but I am equally glad it's over.

"Sex is fine," he concluded, "but love is better."

Instead of sexual experimentation, Ossie and Ruby decided to explore other aspects of their personalities and talents. Ossie tried directing; in 1970, his *Cotton Comes to Harlem* was one of the first successful Hollywood films aimed at a black market. Ruby tried writing; she adapted several stories and novels for television. The most successful of these was "Zora Is My Name!," a dramatization of the works of the Harlem Renaissance writer Zora Neale Hurston, which PBS's Masterpiece Theater presented in 1983. She also wrote and in 1996 and 1998 starred in a one-woman play, *My One Good Nerve*.

Together, the two hosted a successful radio show, "The Ossie Davis and Ruby Dee Story Hour," in the seventies, and a television show, "With Ossie and Ruby," in the eighties.

In contrast to their open marriage, these experiments proved a boon not just to their careers but to their relationship. As Ossie put it: "When I met her, I had not known that she was a writer and humorist; I had not thought about her being the kind of performer she is until other people—critics and so forth—expressed their appreciation of her. . . . Then she becomes attractive to someone else, and you say, 'Oh, don't go yet. Let me take another look at you.' And you appreciate her in a new way."

Ruby added, "Marriage becomes a process rather than an accomplishment or a fact. It goes on and on. You keep on getting married."

7

Paul Newman and Joanne Woodward

*A*gainst a background where marriages seem just another special effect, Paul Newman and Joanne Woodward have stood out as a symbol of middle-American stability. For more than forty years, they have been the most un-Hollywood of Hollywood couples, shunning publicity and California for the quiet of suburban Connecticut.

When Woodward won the Oscar for best actress, she shocked Hollywood by appearing at the Academy Awards in a simple dress she had made herself. Said Joan Collins, only half-jokingly, "Joanne Woodward has set Hollywood glamour back twenty-five years."

An evening with the Newmans was equally unglamorous, as Paul described it: "Three or four nights a week I cook up a batch of popcorn and open a couple of beers, and read a book. That's what I call gracious living."

Was Newman ever tempted to stray? "I have steak at home," he once responded. "Why go out for hamburger?"

It was not a remark that would endear him to feminists, especially since he went on to call Woodward "the best of the big-time broads." But it secured their image as an average American couple who just happened to be movie stars.

The reality, as usual, was more complicated.

&*— *&

Paul and Joanne first met in October 1952 at the offices of MCA, the agency that represented both of them. They got to know each other better a month later, when both were cast in the Pulitzer Prize–winning play *Picnic.*

Paul wanted the part of the lead, but the director Joshua Logan thought—difficult as it now is to believe—that he wasn't sexy enough. Instead, Paul landed a secondary role and became understudy for the lead. Joanne was understudy for two other roles.

Recalled Logan: "He went into the understudy rehearsal every day and danced with Joanne Woodward. . . . He was such a clean-cut, well-put-together boy that I said, 'Now, you've got to learn how to be a little "dirtier" . . . wiggle your ass a little bit when you're dancing.'

"I think it did Paul a lot of good," Logan continued, "and I *know* it did Joanne Woodward good. Joanne and he, I guess, got to know each other very well."

Everyone could see Paul and Joanne were attracted to each other. The problem was, not only was Paul already married, but his wife, Jackie Witte, was about to give birth to their second child.

Paul and Joanne resolved not to see each other; however, they continued to run into each other. Even after *Picnic* closed, they traveled in the same circles, first in New York and then in Hollywood.

For Paul, who felt trapped in his marriage, the tensions led to drinking, a problem that manifested itself in 1956 when he was arrested in Long Island for leaving the scene of an accident after he destroyed a fire hydrant and some shrubbery.

Joanne, herself a child of divorced parents, did not want to be responsible for breaking up Paul's marriage. She became engaged briefly to writer James Costigan, but she remained close with—and strongly attracted to—Paul.

Things heated up in 1957, when Paul and Joanne were cast as costars in *The Long Hot Summer*. Jackie, understandably suspicious, packed up the kids and went home to her mother in Wisconsin. Paul and Joanne moved into a house in Malibu Beach, which they shared with their friends, writer Gore Vidal and his companion, Howard Austen.

Joanne, by now, was getting impatient, but Paul was still reluctant to leave Jackie and their now three kids. So Joanne—according to Vidal—pulled out one of the oldest tricks in the book: to make Paul jealous, she became engaged to Vidal.

In his memoirs, Vidal wrote: "Joanne Woodward and I were nearly married, but that was at her insistence and based entirely on her passion not for me but Paul Newman. Paul was taking his time about divorcing his first wife, and Joanne calculated, shrewdly as it proved, that the possibility of our marriage would give him the needed push. It did."

In January 1958, Paul and Joanne appeared together on live television in *The Eighty-Yard Run*. Two weeks later, having gotten a quickie Mexican divorce from Jackie, Paul married Joanne.

"I felt guilty as hell," Paul said about the divorce, "and will carry that guilt for the rest of my life."

❦— —❧

In 1957, when Joanne won the Oscar for her performance as the multiple-personality heroine in *The Three Faces of Eve*, it was the only point in her career that she was a bigger star than Paul.

Actress Patricia Neal explained, "She was a very pretty, young, talented girl. But *movie star* is different. Paul, you know, *movie star*. But Joanne did it on acting ability, because that part was incredibly challenging."

Joanne put it this way: "I think a movie star is someone people recognize on the street. They go to see her movies whether the reviews are good or not. . . . I just don't feel like a movie star."

Paul of course was. With such hits as *Cat on a Hot Tin Roof* in 1958, *Exodus* in 1960, *The Hustler* in 1961, and *Hud* in 1963, he was soon a star by anyone's definition.

Publicly, Joanne expressed relief that her career seemed to have peaked so early. Indeed, neither Joanne nor Paul was ever comfortable living the life of a Hollywood star. Gossip columnist Hedda Hopper, with obvious consternation, wrote: "They bought no property, lived in a simple home without swimming pool, on a month-to-month basis, and drove rented cars."

Paul made no secret of what he thought about the Hollywood lifestyle. "Here's what happens," he said. "You start making more money than you have ever thought existed. First you buy a mansion so big that even the rooms have rooms. Your children have to have individual governesses . . . Comes April 15 and the income-tax people want $200,000. You call your agent but the only scripts available are real dogs. You have to take them any-how. Either that or fire a couple of governesses."

It was no surprise, then, when the couple moved from Hol-lywood to suburban Westport, Connecticut, and attempted to preserve their privacy with a sign on the front gate that read: "Please—they have moved—the Piersons."

When Joanne did emerge from behind that gate, it was mostly to accompany Paul on location and occasionally to act alongside him. Her life was that of a suburban housewife; she took care of their three children and sometimes the three from Paul's mar-riage to Jackie. And she took care of Paul. Not only did she sew her own Oscar gown, but she knitted her husband's sweaters—thirty-seven of them in their first year of marriage alone.

Underneath, however, Joanne could not help but resent how her once-promising career had been subordinated to Paul's. Years later, she said: "If I had to do it all over again, I would make the decision one way or another. My career has suffered because of the children, and my children have suffered because of my career. And that's not fair."

Another time, Joanne admitted that "a lot of mornings I can hardly make myself get out from under the covers and try to be me. I've had times when I figured the best thing Paul could do with me is to take me out in back and shoot me like a crippled horse. That's how 'fulfilled' I am."

His chauvinistic remark about steak and hamburger notwith-standing, Paul was not oblivious to his wife's sacrifices. In an interview with Gloria Steinem, he said: "I know she misses out on things, Broadway plays for instance. . . . Sometimes I come home and here's this woman wandering around the house muttering, 'What-am-I-doing-cooking-for-seven-people-what-the-hell-am-I-doing?'"

In 1962, Joanne read a script that she thought would make a fine vehicle for her and Paul. Paul recalled their ensuing conversation: "I read it and said, 'Joanne, it's just a bunch of one-liners.' And she said, 'You son of a bitch, I've been carting your children around, taking care of them at the expense of my career, taking care of you and your house.' And I said, 'That's what I said. It's a terrific script. I can't think of anything I'd rather do.'"

Unfortunately, Paul's analysis of the script turned out to be correct. *A New Kind of Love*, like most of the other movies in which the couple had appeared together, flopped.

In 1967, it was time to try something new. Joanne was tired of acting with Paul; Paul was tired of acting, period. She wanted another shot at stardom; he was sick of it, even as his latest movie, *Cool Hand Luke*, was on its way to becoming another hit.

Joanne explained: "Now I'd like to be more active, principally because I feel I've done my bit for the population explosion and raised the children to where I feel I'm not depriving them if I'm working."

And as for Paul, he decided that "if blue eyes are what it's about, and not the accumulation of my work as a professional actor, I may as well turn in my union card right now and go into gardening."

Paul and Joanne decided to work together again, but this time with Paul behind the camera. The movie they selected, *Rachel, Rachel*, was a risky venture. Paul had never directed before, and the couple had to put up their own money. Both were putting their self-esteem on the line, but the results pleased them. "I wasn't really quite sure how it was going to turn out," she said. "Now I think he is the best director I have ever worked with—and not just because he's my husband."

The New York Film Critics Circle voted Paul best director and Joanne best actress. The Academy nominated her for best actress and the movie for best picture. Though neither won, *Rachel, Rachel* had accomplished its purpose.

Joanne had reestablished herself as a first-rate actress, and Paul had proven there were brains behind those blue eyes.

A year after *Rachel, Rachel* brought them triumphantly together, Paul and Joanne costarred in a movie that would pull them apart. In *Winning*, Paul played a race car driver and Joanne his wife. Neither was particularly good, nor was the movie.

But the real impact of *Winning* was that it ignited Paul's passion for car racing. He had always been a fan, but now, though forty-four years old, he was intent on becoming a competitive racer. Every weekend, Paul would head off to the track, leaving Joanne worrying whether he'd come back alive.

Paul tried directing Joanne again in the 1972 movie *The Effect of Gamma Rays on Man-in-the-Moon Marigolds*, but this time they fought on the set. Joanne played an embittered widow named Beatrice. "The role had an effect on me both during the shooting and afterwards," she later said. "At home, I was a monster, and Paul and I avoided each other as much as possible. There was something ugly about the character of Beatrice that got to me. . . . I understood her all too well."

That may be true, but one suspects the underlying problem was that Joanne resented Paul's frequent absences, this time as he headed to the track instead of to Hollywood. On top of being left with the children, she was now left worrying about his safety.

Paul was remarkably successful as a racer, especially considering his age. In 1976, he won the Sports Car Club of America President's Cup, the highest honor for an amateur driver. Then, to Joanne's dismay, he decided to turn pro.

Almost inevitably, there were accidents, and while Paul was never seriously injured, he had enough close calls to justify Joanne's fears. In 1980, when his brakes failed at 140 miles per hour, he crashed into a wall.

But the worst accident, from Joanne's viewpoint, was in 1983, if only because she was there to witness it. A photographer watched her confront him afterwards in the pit. "One look said it all," he recalled. "It was like 'Thank God you're alive!' and at the same time 'Why are you doing this?'"

Paul considered giving up racing, but it was now more important to him than acting. Joanne's response, he said, was "Do what you want, but I've finished my obligations."

So Joanne left the track to Paul and delved into interests of her own—in particular, ballet. She was too old to become a ballerina, but she became an active board member and financial backer for a ballet company called Dancers.

The arrangement worked for both. "We like each other a lot. We have great respect for each other. We've known each other a long time and we feel very comfortable together," Joanne said. "We don't believe in being together all the time."

Paul agreed. "Wives *shouldn't* feel obligated to accompany their husbands to a ball game, husbands *do* look a bit silly attending morning coffee breaks with the neighborhood wives. Husbands and wives *should* have separate interests, cultivate different sets of friends. . . . You can't spend a lifetime breathing down each other's necks.

"We have a deal," he added. "I trade her a couple of ballets for a couple of races."

↬•— —•↬

In November 1978, Paul's oldest son died of a drug overdose. Scott was Jackie's son, not Joanne's, and by some accounts he had never recovered from his parents' divorce. He was jealous of his half-sisters, who grew up in luxury, while he and Jackie's two daughters had a more middle-class life.

Paul and Joanne wanted to shield their children—all of them, not just Jackie's—from the Hollywood lifestyle, just as they themselves chose Connecticut over California. But Paul later recognized that he had sent the kids mixed messages.

"I was all over the place, too loving one minute, too distant the next," he said. "One day they were flying on the Concorde, and the next day they were expected to do their own laundry. It was very hard for them to get a balance."

Joanne, cast in the role of stepmother, couldn't help. She feared Scott was just using his father for his money or his contacts, such as when Paul got him a bit part in *The Towering Inferno* (in which Paul starred). "Scott and I didn't speak for several years," Joanne recalled. "He was going through difficult times, and I resented the fact that he wasn't standing on his own feet and was using Paul. That made me angry, for Paul."

By the time of Scott's death, father and son were barely speaking either, though Paul had arranged for psychologists to be on call twenty-four hours a day, in case Scott wanted help. It was one of these psychologists who found Scott in a West Los Angeles motel, but too late.

The death was officially ruled accidental, but many suspected suicide. Scott's acting career had gone nowhere after *Inferno*, and an attempt at a singing career had also stalled. He was living a dangerous life, drinking excessively, taking a variety of drugs, and also skydiving—the last perhaps an attempt to match his father's daredevil racing.

Paul's first reaction to Scott's death was to throw himself all the more into racing and also to drown his despair and guilt in drink. "It's an event that never gets better. It gets different but never gets better," he said.

But Paul survived, as did his marriage. The couple continued to work together on an occasional movie, as well as on Newman's Own, a food company Paul founded which grew into a multimillion-dollar business. Paul donated all the profits to charity.

Paul and Joanne also donated time and money to the Scott Newman Foundation, which friends of the couple founded to support antidrug activities. Joanne served on the board and Paul underwrote some of the films the foundation produced.

The foundation gave not only Paul and Joanne but Hollywood a chance to prevent others from dying as Scott had. That was fitting, for though it would be unfair and simplistic to blame Hollywood for Scott's death, it certainly played a role in it.

Paul and Joanne had moved a continent away from Hollywood, and they did indeed create a very un-Hollywood marriage. But they could not keep Scott from dreaming of California and from going there to live—and die.

8

Richard Burton and Elizabeth Taylor

*I*n the 1963 movie *Cleopatra*, both Rome and Egypt are in the midst of civil wars, the former's between the forces of Caesar and Pompey, the latter's between those of Cleopatra and Ptolemy. Caesar arrives at the palace of Ptolemy, where a peddler presents him with a rug. Caesar unrolls the rug and finds Cleopatra inside. The two strike a deal: Caesar helps Cleopatra defeat Ptolemy, and later she joins him for his triumphant return home. Cleopatra, wrapped in gold, arrives in Rome on a giant model of a sphinx, from which she descends to greet Caesar.

Yet the affair of Cleopatra and Caesar pales before the love of Cleopatra and Antony. With Caesar assassinated, Rome is again plunged into civil war, this time between the legions of Octavian and Antony. Antony, following in Caesar's footsteps, arrives in Egypt. He storms into Cleopatra's bedchamber, taking Caesar's place as her ally and lover. But this time their enemies pursue and defeat them. Antony has no choice but to fall on his sword.

On learning of her lover's death, Cleopatra puts her hand in a basket of figs which she knows conceals a poisonous snake. "The taste of these, they say, is sharp and swiftly over," she says, dying. "Antony . . . Antony, wait."

It was, perhaps the most famous love affair of all time. And yet, by the time the movie came out, no one paid much attention to Antony and Cleopatra. Instead, the world's attention was focused—almost entirely, it sometimes seemed—on the actor and actress who played them: Richard Burton and Elizabeth Taylor.

In the beginning, what caught everyone's attention was the scandal, or "le scandale" as Burton dubbed it. After all, both Burton and Taylor were married; he was still with his first wife, and she was up to her fourth husband.

Taylor's reputation had just barely recovered from the scandal of her latest marriage, this one to singer Eddie Fisher. Fisher had been the best friend of Mike Todd, Taylor's third husband, who was killed in a plane crash in 1958. It was unseemly enough that Todd's widow and best friend took up with each other right after his death. What made it far worse was that at the time they began seeing each other, Fisher was still married to Debbie Reynolds, whose girl-next-door image was in sharp contrast to Elizabeth's femme fatale.

Taylor didn't help her situation any in a telephone interview with the columnist Hedda Hopper. When Hopper asked her what Todd would have thought of her relationship with Fisher, she replied, "What do you expect me to do? Sleep alone?"

Taylor's image rebounded in March 1961, amid some early filming of *Cleopatra*. She was rushed to a London hospital with a life-threatening congestion of the lungs. When she emerged from the hospital, she was no longer a husband-stealing wicked widow. Like Cleopatra, she was now a heroic fighter against the odds; if she loved more than one man, well, that too fit the queen's image.

Enter Burton.

The part of Mark Antony was originally to be played by Stephen Boyd, but delays in filming (partly because of Taylor's illness) forced a change. Now the part belonged to Burton, the eminent Shakespearean actor best known for starring on Broadway in *Camelot*. The scene shifted from London to Rome, where *Cleopatra* was to recommence shooting.

On January 22, 1962, the couple filmed their first scenes together, and it was immediately clear that they weren't just playing at being in love. The director, Joseph Mankiewicz, called "Action," and the two kissed. They were still kissing when Mankiewicz said, "Would you mind if I say cut?"

Elizabeth's version was that she immediately found Richard sympathetic because he was so hung over that he was shaking on the set and could barely remember his lines. Richard fell for her, according to some of his friends, right after seeing Elizabeth naked in the bathing scene.

More cynical observers saw Taylor as a pampered Hollywood superstar who took what—and who—she wanted, regardless of the consequences. As for Burton, they said, his conscience did not stand in the way once he saw the chance to turn himself from a respected, but by no means wealthy, stage actor into a Hollywood superstar.

Lawrence Olivier cabled Burton asking whether he wanted to be a great actor or a household name.

"Both," he answered.

Eddie Fisher, obviously not the most objective reporter, cast an even harsher light on Burton's ambitions. Fisher recalled meeting Richard one day on the outskirts of Rome.

"You don't need her," Burton told Fisher (or so said Eddie). "You're a star already. She's going to make me a star."

But these stories were not entirely fair. For there was also no question that Elizabeth and Richard were genuinely and passionately attracted to each other. Both were, after all, extremely attractive; both loved sex; and both were risking a great deal of public contempt to be with the other. Each found the other endlessly fascinating, as did the public.

Indeed, so determined was Elizabeth to hold on to Richard that when he told her he was going back to his wife, Sybil, Elizabeth took an overdose of sleeping pills. On February 17, she had to be rushed to the hospital in Rome. The studio described the incident as food poisoning, but many suspected it was a suicide attempt. In any case, Richard quickly returned to her side.

The reaction to the Taylor-Burton romance made the Taylor-Fisher publicity seem tame. As Elizabeth herself recalled in her memoir: "Perhaps not since the time of Cleopatra has a love affair elicited such intense interest and scrutiny from a civilized world."

In England, the *Daily Mirror* called Elizabeth "one long eruption of matrimonial agitation." In the United States, *Life* magazine's story included a picture of Elizabeth's children with the caption: "Please, Who's My Daddy Now?"

Twentieth Century-Fox later joined the fray, unsuccessfully suing Taylor and Burton for $50 million on the grounds that their "deplorable and amoral conduct" violated the studio's morals clause.

Even Congress got involved. A member of the House of Representatives, Iris Blitch, called for Congress to ban from the country "those who show no concern for either the flag or people and show no respect for cherished institutions or God." Commented Taylor's biographer, Donald Spoto: "One can only imagine what Elizabeth and Richard did with her name."

In March 1962, Fisher held a press conference in New York. Gamely, he tried to impress the reporters by calling Taylor in Rome so she could publicly deny the rumors. "Well, Eddie," said Elizabeth, who was accused of many things but never dishonesty, "I can't actually do that because there is, you see, some truth in the rumors."

In April 1963, Richard divorced Sybil, paying her about $1.5 million. Even those convinced his relationship with Elizabeth was all about money had to concede she cost him pretty much all the money he had at that point.

Just under a year later, Eddie granted Elizabeth a divorce. The stage was now set for the Taylor-Burton wedding, and on March 13, 1964, the couple announced they would be married in two days. The ceremony took place at a Montreal hotel. It was

Elizabeth's fifth marriage and Richard's second. Quipped her friend Oscar Levant: "Always a bride, never a bridesmaid." He also dubbed Elizabeth "the other woman of the year."

More hopeful than Levant, Burton took the stage the next day in Toronto, where he was starring in *Hamlet*. After a final curtain call, he called Taylor onto the stage and addressed both his bride and the audience. Quoting one of Hamlet's lines to Ophelia, he said, "I say we will have no more marriages."

The marriage lessened the scandal but not the attention. The public continued to be fascinated by the couple, especially by their royal lifestyle. Over the next ten years, Burton and Taylor earned almost $90 million from their movies and spent more than $65 million. They bought a fleet of Rolls-Royces; paintings by Monet, Picasso, van Gogh, and Rembrandt; and a yacht. And when the first yacht was in dry dock and British authorities informed them they couldn't bring their dogs ashore until they had passed through quarantine, the couple rented a second yacht for the dogs.

Richard and Elizabeth had become the poster children for self-indulgence. Elizabeth arrived at a London banquet wearing the 69.42-carat Cartier diamond, for which the couple had paid $1.5 million. Princess Margaret, seated beside her, looked at the diamond and said, "How very vulgar!"

"Yes," Elizabeth answered. "Ain't it great?"

They also reigned in Hollywood. In 1965, the couple starred brilliantly in *Who's Afraid of Virginia Woolf?*—Edward Albee's tragicomic play about George and Martha, a husband and wife who torture each other during a drunken dinner party. Taylor was especially impressive, courageously taking on the role of a disheveled middle-aged matron.

The next year, Taylor and Burton again played a volatile couple to perfection, this time in Franco Zeffirelli's version of *The Taming of the Shrew*. "It's a joyous romp," wrote Sheridan Morley of *Shrew*. "On the screen the Burtons managed to convey a kind of infectious delight in brawling their way into bed."

Alas, in their real lives, the brawling would gradually eclipse the loving. Soon their lives would resemble those of the hapless George and Martha rather than the ribald Petruchio and Katharina.

⟪⟶ ⟶⟫

After *Woolf* and *Shrew*, their collaborations quickly slid downhill. There was a string of artistic and commercial failures, among them *The Comedians* (1967) and *Boom* (1968). Critics tore into the movies and the couple. "They don't so much act as deign to appear before us and there is neither dignity nor discipline in what they do," said *Life* about *Boom*. "She is fat . . . He acts with nothing but his voice, rolling out his lines with much elegance, but with no feeling at all."

Richard had always been a heavy drinker; by the late sixties, he was drinking even more. Elizabeth was drinking and taking all sorts of prescription drugs, as well as gaining a lot of weight.

Richard and Elizabeth seemed to have become George and Martha.

"We are fighting and have been fighting for over a year now over anything and everything," Richard wrote in an August 1969 diary entry.

Now the extravagance of their lifestyle could not conceal the bitterness of their lives. His friends blamed her for corrupting the heir to Olivier, turning Richard from the most promising Shakespearean actor of his generation into an overpaid movie hack. Her friends blamed him for boozing both of them into oblivion. Both their friends were right: however much Richard and Elizabeth loved each other, they also brought out the worst in each other.

In February 1973, ABC broadcast a two-part television movie starring the couple in the all-too-appropriately titled *Divorce His, Divorce Hers*. It looked at the dissolution of a marriage from the point of view of each member of the couple. Life imitated art: Richard and Elizabeth separated in July, briefly reconciled in December, then divorced in June 1974.

That was not the end of their story, of course. Richard stopped drinking and the couple reconciled again in August 1975, then remarried in October. The wedding (her sixth, his third) took place in a remote village in Botswana, witnessed mostly by African wildlife. "Sturm has remarried Drang and all is right with the world," wrote Ellen Goodman in the *Boston Globe*.

But Richard immediately started drinking again, and less than ten months later, they were again divorced. "I love Richard Burton with every fiber of my soul," Elizabeth said. "But we can't be together. We're too mutually self-destructive."

Richard agreed. In 1982—by this time he was separated from his third wife, Susan Hunt, and Elizabeth from her sixth husband, John Warner—Richard escorted Elizabeth to her fiftieth birthday party in London. But he quickly squelched press speculation about a reunion. "The best way for Elizabeth and myself to keep each other together is to be apart," he said.

Two years later, Richard died of a cerebral hemorrhage. Richard's fourth wife, Sally Hay, asked Elizabeth not to attend the funeral because her arrival would surely shatter the solemnity of the occasion. But five days later, Elizabeth quietly visited Richard's grave.

It was one of the few times she was with him without the world looking on.

9

Christopher and Dana Reeve

*T*he headline was irresistible, and it was the British tabloids that first announced the Monday after Memorial Day 1995: "Superman Breaks His Back." American newspapers were short-staffed until after the holiday weekend, but they quickly followed up with stories about how actor Christopher Reeve, best known for playing the Man of Steel in the late seventies and early eighties, was paralyzed and perhaps near death in a Virginia hospital after being thrown from a horse during a show-jumping competition.

The irony was greater than any tabloid headline could express. Chris Reeve had lived a life that was, if not actually faster than a speeding bullet, remarkably active physically. He was a pilot, a sailor, a bicyclist, a skier, a windsurfer, a scuba diver, and a mountain climber. Riding was his latest passion, one he'd taken up in 1984 when he played a cavalry captain in the movie *Anna Karenina*.

Chris had become an accomplished—yet careful—rider. Indeed, he had just posed for a safety poster that had urged riders to wear helmets. The copy read: "In films I play an invincible hero. But in real life I wouldn't think of riding without a helmet."

The accident that Saturday afternoon was not his fault. Chris's horse, Buck, started to jump a fence, then seemed to stop in midair. Some witnesses thought a rabbit spooked him; others blamed shadows. Chris landed on the top rail, then fell on his forehead. He lay motionless on the ground. He was

taken to the local hospital in Culpeper, Virginia, then flown—
in a helicopter named Pegasus, after the flying horse of Greek
mythology—to the University of Virginia Medical Center in
Charlottesville.

Chris did not become fully conscious for five days. When he
did, doctors explained the situation: his first and second cervi-
cal vertebrae were fractured. Not only would he not walk again,
but he wouldn't be able to use his arms or breathe without being
hooked up to a ventilator.

Chris's response, he recalled in his autobiography, was to
wonder: "Why not die and save everyone a lot of trouble?"

At that point, Chris's wife, Dana, came into the hospital room.
"She stood beside me, and we made eye contact," Chris wrote.
"I mouthed my first lucid words to her: 'Maybe we should let
me go.'"

Dana did not hesitate for a second. "I am only going to say
this once," she answered. "I will support whatever you do,
because this is your life, and your decision. But I want you to
know that I'll be with you for the long haul, no matter what."

Then she added, "You're still you. And I love you."

These were the words, Chris said, that saved his life.

⟪•— •⟫

Chris did not meet Dana until 1987, when he was thirty-five.
Until then, he was cynical about marriage. He prided himself on
his independence; this manifested itself not just in his choice of

sports—many of which stressed individual achievements—but in his love life as well. When he met Dana, he already had two children with former model Gae Exton, but he and Gae had never married. They'd separated amicably earlier that year.

Chris traced his attitude about marriage back to his childhood. His parents divorced when he was just three. Each then remarried but their second marriages were also troubled.

"All my life I had heard people say that they loved each other and that they would be together forever, to have and to hold from this day forward, and so forth, and then it would turn out not to be true," Chris wrote. "Or irreconcilable differences would emerge.

"My father had an affair. My stepfather often would not come home," he continued. "I concluded that in most cases marriage is a sham."

Chris remained close to his mother, but his relationship with Franklin Reeve, a distinguished poet and scholar, was increasingly distant. When Chris landed the role of Superman, he called his father, who took him out to dinner and ordered champagne to celebrate. Chris was thrilled to see his father so excited.

But the excitement quickly faded when his father realized Chris had been cast as the comic-book superhero. Franklin Reeve had thought his son was going to star in George Bernard Shaw's play *Man and Superman*.

Chris's independence had its upside, of course, especially as he carved out a career in theater and films. After the success of the Superman movies, he refused to allow himself to be type-cast as a superhero, even if it meant turning down big money and instead sometimes narrating documentaries or audio books he believed in. By the time he met Dana, he was no longer on Hollywood's A-list.

They met at the Williamstown Theater Festival in Massa-chusetts, where Chris was acting and Dana was singing. Chris found himself not just in love, but believing in love for the first time. "She rescued me when I was lying in Virginia with a bro-ken body, but that was really the second time," he wrote. "The first time she rescued me was the night we met."

Actually, it wasn't quite that simple.

"I still couldn't get past the issue of marriage," Chris con-ceded. By 1990, they were living together in New York, with Dana increasingly itchy about Chris's unwillingness to commit. A year later, she threatened to leave him, and he agreed to go into therapy.

"I finally talked through everything I had always feared about marriage," he said. In April 1992, Chris and Dana returned to Williamstown for their wedding. They pledged to remain together—in sickness and in health.

"I got the better part of the deal," Chris wrote.

❦⋅—⋅❧

Dana didn't see the accident. She was home with their three-year-old son, Will. When she arrived at the Culpeper hospital, she didn't know how seriously her husband was injured, though she was certainly worried when she saw the helicopter take off. "That's not for a broken arm," she thought.

Still, Dana remained calm. A doctor's daughter, she had a great deal of faith in medical expertise. And she had Will with her, so she had to remain in control as she drove from Culpeper to Charlottesville.

At the hospital, she spoke to Chris's doctor and to her father. Neither offered much in the way of hope. There was no cure for a spinal cord injury. Chris was paralyzed for life.

The doctors had to perform a tricky operation that would, essentially, reattach Chris's head to his spinal column, but that would at most let him shrug his shoulders and perhaps breathe on his own for short periods of time. He would not be able to move his arms or legs, he would not have any control over his bowel or bladder movements or his sexual function.

"We left an able-bodied existence full of privilege and ease and entered a life of disability, with all its accompanying restrictions and challenges," Dana wrote. "We went from the 'haves' to the 'have-nots.'"

Neither Dana nor Chris practiced any traditional religion, and they now faced a situation that would have tested anyone's faith. "We are good people," Dana later wrote. "Why had we been punished in this way?"

For Dana, as for Chris, love provided the strength to go on. Not just their love for each other, but from many others. It came pouring in, in the form of messages from around the world. Letters came from Bill Clinton and Nancy Reagan, from Hugh Grant and Emma Thompson, from Katharine Hepburn and Robert DeNiro. Princess Diana wrote to Chris, reminding him of when they had danced together and hoping they would do so again.

Chris compared breaking his neck to entering a dark tunnel. When he received the letters, he said, "Suddenly there was light."

Many came from other paralyzed people, offering hope and advice. Margot Kidder, who had played Lois Lane to Chris's Superman and who had spent two years in a wheelchair after a 1990 car crash, wrote that he should never give up, no matter what.

The town of Metropolis, Illinois, with a population of sixty-seven hundred, sent an eight-foot postcard signed by more than five thousand residents. All told, the Reeves received more than four hundred thousand letters. Some were addressed simply: Superman, USA.

What accounted for the outpouring? "Superman is a traditional archetype in our culture," Dana told the *Los Angeles Times* in 1999. "If he could succumb to the frailties of mortal man, what's to become of the rest of us?"

Dana sifted through the letters and read many of them to Chris in the hospital, and later in a rehabilitation center and at home. "As I listened, I soon understood something new," Chris recalled. "These letters were not from strangers, just people I had never met. . . . We are only strangers if we choose to look away."

❦⚬—⚬❧

Neither Chris nor Dana looked away. After the accident, they devoted much of their time to the search for a cure for paralysis. Their goal was that Chris and other quadriplegics would someday walk again. They founded the Christopher Reeve Foundation to raise money for research, and both have hosted fund-raisers, lobbied in Washington, and spoken around the country.

The research has resulted in some breakthroughs, though no cure. In 1996, rats whose spinal cords had been cut were able to move their hind limbs after scientists grafted tiny bridges made of cells taken from peripheral nerves. "I never thought I'd be jealous of a rodent," Chris said. Other scientists have found that nerves in the spinal cord can be made to regenerate, bringing more hope for a cure.

In 2000, Chris appeared in an ad for Nuveen Investments that aired during the Super Bowl. In the ad, to the shock of many viewers, he stands up and walks stiffly onto a stage. The feat was accomplished solely by computers and editing.

Some advocates of paralyzed people strongly criticized Chris for raising false hopes. Even Dana expressed some doubts about the ad. She told the *Daily News*: "I didn't like it because I worried that the commercial would result in disabled people being carried away by this fantasy of dramatic recovery. I would rather see the emphasis go toward improving their care and their quality of life."

But Chris defended the ad and remains adamant that he and other paralyzed people should never give up the dream of walking again. "Everything in that commercial will one day be possible," he said.

Meanwhile, both Chris and Dana, in addition to devoting themselves to the cause, resumed their careers. Dana continued to sing and act, and in 2000 cohosted a Lifetime cable TV show. Unlike many in her position, she was able to draw on the couple's insurance and savings to pay a staff of nurses and aides that provides Chris with the twenty-four-hour care he needs. "We considered ourselves very lucky," Chris commented. "In many cases the patient's spouse has to become the primary caregiver, and the stress on the marriage is intense."

But, even if she wasn't his nurse, in what sense could she remain his lover? Dana told the *Times*, "Obviously, sex isn't what it used to be. We always had a great sex life, so that's a tremendous loss. We're still as intimate as we used to be. We just lock the door and turn the monitor off. We refuse to become roommates."

The couple thought of having a baby, which might still have been possible through artificial insemination. But in the end, they decided it would be too painful for Chris to raise another child without being able to hold him or her.

Chris returned to acting in 1998, starring as a man in a wheelchair in a remake of *Rear Window*. He also directed an HBO movie, *In the Gloaming*, about an AIDS patient who goes home to die.

On their wedding anniversary, Dana wrote Chris: "This path we are on is unpredictable, mysterious, profoundly challenging, and yes, even fulfilling. . . . I have no regrets."

She added: "Our future will be bright, my darling one."

ROYALS AND RULERS

10

Edith and Woodrow Wilson

Some called her the "presidentress" or "the first woman president." Others were more snide, such as the senator who called hers a "petticoat government." Even her defenders could not deny that Edith Wilson, the wife of President Woodrow Wilson, wielded unprecedented power.

For the three months starting October 2, 1919—when her husband suffered a stroke and she found him on the floor of a White House bathroom, paralyzed on the left side—the president's wife was the only one, besides his doctors, allowed to see him. Every aide was barred, every cabinet member, even the vice president.

In her memoir, she recalled what she referred to as her "stewardship": "I studied every paper, sent from the different Secretaries or Senators and tried to digest and present in tabloid form the things that, despite my vigilance, had to go to the President.

"I, myself, never made a single decision regarding the disposition of public affairs," she continued. "The only decision that was mine was what was important and what was not and the *very* important decision of when to present matters to my husband."

Edith could not possibly have been as naive as she presented herself. She was fully aware that her decisions as to what matters went before the president determined what actions the government could take during his illness. She was the most powerful person in the country, and she knew it.

The question asked then (and long after) was: why did she do it?

Was she, as her detractors charged, a hugely ambitious woman who seized control of the government at a time when women didn't even have the right to vote? Or was she a loyal aide, desperately trying to protect her husband's dream of establishing a League of Nations as set forth in the Treaty of Versailles?

Edith's answer to the question was simple: what she did, she did for love. "I asked the doctors to be frank with me," she wrote in her memoir. "They all said that as the brain was as clear as ever . . . there was every reason to think recovery possible . . . But recovery could not be hoped for, they said, unless the President were released from every disturbing problem."

Naturally, she asked the doctor whether it wouldn't therefore be better for the president to resign. Vice President Thomas Marshall could take over, and Woodrow Wilson could get the rest he needed.

"No," the doctor said (according to Edith). "For Mr. Wilson to resign would have . . . a serious effect on our patient. He has staked his life and made his promise to the world to do all in his power to get the treaty ratified. If he resigns, the greatest incentive to recovery is gone."

So, Edith explained, she followed the doctor's advice. She ran the country, not to satisfy her own ambitions or even those of her husband, but because it was the best way to ensure the patient's recovery. She was not driven by power or by patriotism, but by love.

❦——❧

Of *his* love for her, there could be no doubt.

The two had met in April 1915, less than a year after the death of his first wife, Ellen. They were introduced by his cousin, Helen Woodrow Bones. At the time, Edith was forty-two, the widow of a prominent Washington jeweler. Woodrow was fifty-eight and the president.

Their courtship was constrained by his office. He could not go out in public unaccompanied by the Secret Service, and even then the press carefully followed the private life of the president, especially a newly widowed one. That meant he courted her largely by letter, and his letters to her—sometimes several a day—provide a clear picture of a man passionately in love.

"You are so beautiful!" he wrote in one. "I have learned what you are and my heart is wholly enthralled."

Another said: "How deep I have drunk of the sweet fountains of love that are in you . . . how full of life and every sweet perfection!"

Yet another: "It does not make me proud to think of myself as the beloved President of 100 million people . . . but it does make me proud to think of myself as the accepted and trusted lover of the sweet lady whom I adore."

On May 4, just a few weeks after he first met her, the president asked Edith to marry him.

Edith was not so sure about marriage. She told him, quite reasonably, that they had not known each other long enough. There were also hints in her letters that she had doubts about whether she was sexually attracted to him. A few days after he proposed, for example, Edith wrote: "If you, with your wonderful love, can quicken that which has lain dead so long within me, I promise not to shut it out of my heart but to bid it welcome—and come to you with the joy of it in my eyes.

"On the other hand," she continued, "if I am dead (as I believe) you will not blame me for seeking to live even if it means pain in your own tender heart when my pulse refuses to be in unison with yours."

But Woodrow Wilson was not a man easily dissuaded. He continued to devote his energies to courting her, even while he struggled to cope with foreign crises. A few days after his proposal, a German submarine sunk the *Lusitania*, a British ship off the coast of Ireland. Almost 1,200 people, including 128 Americans, died on board.

The sinking threatened to draw the United States into the European war. On May 11, the president wrote Edith: "What a touch of your hand and a look into your eyes would have meant to me of strength and steadfastness as I made the final decision as to what I should say to Germany."

On July 22, having ordered his secretary of war and secretary of the navy to begin the process that would arm the country in preparation for war, the president wrote to her: "In the midst of all these anxieties and perplexities, my precious Darling, only one light burns steadily for me, and that is the light of your dear love."

No wonder the president's closest adviser, Colonel Edward House, was annoyed. "It seems the President is wholly absorbed in this love affair and is neglecting practically everything else," he wrote in his diary.

House was especially worried about the impact the romance would have on the 1916 presidential election. There was nothing as yet scandalous about the relationship, but voters might not look kindly on the president remarrying so soon after his first wife's death.

So House and some of Wilson's other advisers devised a convoluted plot to squelch the romance. In September, they told the president of an anonymous letter informing them that another woman—Mary Hulbert Peck—was threatening to sell some compromising letters about *her* relationship with Wilson.

Peck was, in fact, an old friend of the president. According to some of his biographers, he had a brief affair with her while vacationing in Bermuda in 1907. He had continued to correspond with her since and had recently lent her $7,500—a sizable sum back then.

The anonymous letter did not exist. Wilson's advisers had invented it in the hope that, fearing a scandal, he would put off his plans to marry until after the election. Or perhaps they hoped that Edith would be scared off by the talk of another woman.

In any case, the plot backfired. The president rushed off to Edith's house to tell her everything—about Mary Peck, the money, the threat of a scandal. He then nervously waited for her reply, which arrived by letter on September 19. "This is my pledge, dearest one," she wrote. "I will stand by you—not for duty, not for pity—but for love."

Far from breaking up the romance, the Peck episode brought the couple closer together. On October 8, they announced their engagement, and the president began to visit Edith's house openly. On the way there, one of his Secret Service agents remembered, "We walked briskly, and the President danced off the curbs and up them when we crossed streets."

On December 18, they were married at her house. A cynical Theodore Roosevelt, whom the president had defeated in the 1912 election, remarked, "My wife is dead; long live my wife."

◆•—•◆

With Edith by his side, Woodrow Wilson was prepared to face the world. It was a far more complex and dangerous world than any previous president had faced.

He tried to negotiate a peace between the Allied and Central Powers, but it was an impossible task. In April 1917, after continued German submarine attacks on American ships, he led the nation into World War I. The U.S. intervention provided the Allies with the margin they needed for victory, and in November 1918, the Germans agreed to an armistice.

More challenges lay ahead, however. Having entered "the war to end all wars," Wilson now took it upon himself to create a lasting peace with the League of Nations, a precursor to the United Nations. He faced strong opposition in the Republican-controlled Senate, which had to approve any treaty.

To the Republicans, the League was a trap that would give foreign nations control over American foreign policy, perhaps even over American troops. Having just finished a bloody European war, they wanted—in the words of their 1920 presidential candidate, Warren Harding—a "return to normalcy."

When it became clear that he could not muster the votes needed to ratify the Treaty of Versailles (and the League of Nations), the president decided to go around the Senate and appeal directly to the people. In September 1919, he set off on a grueling nationwide rail tour.

The tour proved too great a strain for him. On September 22, near Salt Lake City, his doctor noted that he was "suffering very serious fatigue." Three days later, outside of Wichita, he called out to Edith that he felt very sick, and his press secretary had to inform the large crowd waiting at the station that the train was returning directly to Washington.

The president had suffered a transient ischemic attack—a warning of a stroke. The stroke followed on October 2, the day Edith found him on the floor of the White House bathroom.

And so began, in the words of one of his most recent (and best) biographers, August Heckscher, "such a cover-up as American history had not known before." His doctors reported that the president's illness was the result of overwork and exhaustion; they didn't mention that he'd suffered a severe stroke.

For three months, Edith governed the country, consulting sometimes with her husband and sometimes with his doctors. At one point, Vice President Marshall showed up at the White House, figuring he ought to check in with the president. Edith quickly dismissed him, telling him that if she could think of anything for him to do, she'd let him know.

Edith also took the opportunity to sever relations between her husband and Colonel House, whose influence she'd resented as far back as the alleged anonymous note about Mary Peck.

Some of this—House's ouster, for example—was undoubtedly a power play on Edith's part. But overall, she seemed far more interested in keeping government officials away from her husband than in getting them to do anything in particular. So for the most part, historians have believed Edith's explanation—that she ran the country for love.

Wrote Heckscher: "Unwilled and only half pursued, a major share in the governance of the country fell to this woman . . . of passionate devotion to her husband. [Her power] was exercised, on the whole, with single-minded concern for the patient's health."

The Democrats, out of party loyalty, were willing to let matters go on this way. And for a while, the Republicans were also remarkably tolerant, perhaps because they realized that an unelected woman in charge, however galling, was a less powerful political opponent than a fully functioning president.

But eventually, the Republicans' patience wore out. In December, on the pretext that they had to know the president's stance on the kidnapping of an American consul in Mexico, they designated Senator Albert Fall, a New Mexico Republican, to discuss the matter with Wilson. Fall's real job was to find out whether the president was competent to remain in office.

On December 6, Edith reluctantly ushered the senator into the Wilson bedroom. The president had been carefully positioned on the bed so that he lay in a shadow, with his paralyzed left arm hidden under a blanket. Fortunately for Wilson, Fall was more interested in talking than listening, so the forty-minute meeting passed without the president having to say much. Most of what he did say was slurred but, Fall had to admit, made sense.

Before leaving, Fall said to the president: "We've been praying for you, sir."

Wilson's response, Edith later reported, was: "Which way, Senator?"

❧·—·❧

Having passed the senator's not-very-stringent test, Woodrow Wilson completed his term in office. Yet one can't help but view Edith's victory, at least from her husband's standpoint, as a Pyrrhic one. If his hope was that by remaining in power he would secure the passage of the Treaty of Versailles and the League of Nations, it was in vain. In November 1919, the Senate rejected both. The United States never did join the League, which was therefore doomed from the start.

Edith Wilson continued to be a prominent guest at the White House during the seven administrations that followed her husband's, and she eventually had the satisfaction of being honored at the international conference that drew up a charter for the United Nations in 1945. But that was not enacted until twenty-one years after Woodrow Wilson died, during which time, of course, a second world war was fought.

If the president had resigned after his stroke, might history have been different? If Marshall had become president, might he have been more willing to compromise with the Republican senators? Might they have been more willing to compromise with Marshall than with their longtime and implacable foe Wilson? Might such a compromise have meant that the United

States would have joined the League of Nations, and that the League might somehow have averted war?

Probably not.

Exhausted by the first world war, Americans became increasingly isolationist. A year after the Republicans defeated the treaty, Warren Harding easily won the 1920 presidential election. It is unlikely that even a healthy Woodrow Wilson, let alone the entirely unproven Thomas Marshall, could have persuaded the requisite two-thirds of the Senate to approve the treaty or persuaded the people that it was in their interest to join the League.

Still, one can't help but wonder what might have happened if Woodrow Wilson had resigned, or if Edith Wilson had cared a little less about his peace of mind and a little more about his desire for peace on earth. But her love for him overpowered all else, so we'll never know.

II

Edward VIII
and Wallis Simpson

The day after becoming the first British king to abdicate, King Edward VIII—now merely the Duke of Windsor—arrived at Windsor Castle, where a temporary radio studio had been set up. Edward's speech, broadcast on December 11, 1936, was heard around the world.

"You all know the reasons which have impelled me to renounce the Throne," explained the former ruler. And, indeed, there were not many among the millions of listeners who didn't have a pretty good idea about why he did so. But for those who might not have seen a newspaper during the preceding weeks, the rest of Edward's speech spelled it out.

"I want you to understand that in making up my mind I did not forget the country or the empire which as Prince of Wales, and lately as king, I have for twenty-five years tried to serve," he continued. "But you must believe me when I tell you that I have found it impossible to carry the heavy burden of responsibility and to discharge my duties as king as I would wish to do without the help and support of the woman I love."

That woman, everyone knew, was Wallis Warfield Simpson, a twice-divorced American who was, depending on who you asked, either a Cinderella to the real-life prince or a witch more interested in capturing the royal fortune than the royal heart. The latter camp, unfortunately for Edward and Wallis, included the king's own family and his top ministers, who made it clear they would not tolerate a marriage that would make Wallis queen of England.

Edward, who had already heard the worst about how Wallis supposedly bewitched and manipulated him, rose to her defense. "The decision I have made has been mine and mine alone," he stressed in his broadcast. "The other person most nearly concerned has tried up to the last to persuade me to take a different course."

Couched this way, the abdication was perhaps the ultimate romantic gesture: a king sacrificing his kingdom for his love. And, as their subsequent marriage outlasted much of the royal and public disapproval, that was how many came to view it. Yet the love between Edward and Wallis was actually far more complex—and more intriguing—than even the duke's most attentive listeners could have realized back in December 1936.

❦— —❧

Wallis Warfield was born in 1896, two years after Edward. Her father belonged to a wealthy old Baltimore family, but he died just five months after her birth. That left her mother and Wallis at the mercy of their Warfield relatives, who tended to treat them as charity cases. A monthly check from Wallis's uncle allowed her to grow up in reasonable comfort, though always surrounded by people considerably more comfortable than she was.

Wallis jumped at her first chance to escape Baltimore, marrying a handsome naval officer named Earl Winfield Spencer when she was twenty. The marriage was stormy from the start; Spencer, Wallis soon discovered, was an alcoholic and sometimes a violent one. She left him in 1921, lived alone for six years, then reconciled with Spencer and joined him in China, where he was then stationed. After a year in China, Wallis left Spencer for good, receiving an uncontested divorce.

Back in Washington, Wallis met her second husband, the much richer and more stable Ernest Simpson. Simpson was married at the time, but this, as Wallis's detractors were quick to point out, was no major impediment for her. As Simpson's first wife later put it, Wallis "was really a very helpful woman. First she helped herself to my clothes and my apartment, and then she helped herself to my husband."

Wallis and Ernest married in 1928 and settled in London, where he worked in the family shipping business. They lived a comfortable upper-middle-class existence, occasionally attending distinctly upper-class parties. At one of these, in December 1930, Wallis became friendly with Thelma Furness, an American heiress married to Lord Furness, a British shipping magnate. Thelma, as Wallis undoubtedly knew, had for the past three years been the mistress of the Prince of Wales, who was still five years away from becoming King Edward VIII.

Thelma was not the first married woman to become the prince's mistress. Edward's greatest love until then had been Freda Dudley Ward, the wife of a member of Parliament. Their affair had been going on since 1918, and they continued to see each other occasionally even after Edward met Thelma. But it was Thelma who was clearly the prince's favorite . . . until she made the mistake of introducing him to Wallis Simpson.

That first meeting took place, according to Edward's memoirs, in 1931, at a party at Thelma's country home. The prince found himself sitting next to Wallis. For lack of anything else to say, he asked her whether the drafty old English homes made her miss America's central heating.

To the dismay of the other guests, Wallis answered that the prince had disappointed her. "Every American woman who comes to England is asked that same question," she told him. "I had hoped for something more original from the Prince of Wales."

Wallis's memoirs presented a somewhat different version of their first meeting. She put it a year earlier, in 1930, and also at Thelma's country house. But according to Wallis, their first conversation took place sometime after she overheard the prince comment about how bad the lighting there made the women look. When he complimented her on her dress, Wallis answered, "I understood that you thought we all looked ghastly."

Actually, neither version of their meeting was accurate. The actual introduction took place in 1920, when Wallis, still married to Spencer, was one of several hundred U.S. Navy wives who attended a reception for the visiting Prince of Wales in San Diego. Neither apparently made much of an impression on the other that time.

The meeting at Thelma's house, whenever it took place and whatever was said, made a much greater impression on the prince. He began visiting the Simpsons at home and going out with them to dinners and parties. At first, they appeared to be a happy threesome, with Ernest as delighted as Wallis to be in the royal social circle. Gradually, Wallis and Edward were more often seen alone.

In 1934, Thelma returned to England after a visit to America, and she quickly noticed that the prince's attitude toward her had changed. At a palace dinner, she watched the prince pick up a piece of salad, then saw Wallis playfully slap his hand. Thelma and Wallis exchanged glances. "And then and there," Thelma recalled, "I knew the 'reason' was Wallis." After that, Thelma dropped out of the prince's life.

By January 1936, when King George V died and the Prince of Wales became King Edward VIII, his relationship with Wallis was keeping most gossip columnists around the world busy. Only in England did the press, in deference to the royal family, remain silent, but there were few, at least among the wealthy, who didn't know something was going on.

Edward's appeal to Wallis was perfectly clear. "He was the open sesame to a new and glittering world that excited me as nothing in my life had ever done before," she wrote in her memoirs. "Trains were held; yachts materialized; the best suites in the finest hotels were flung open. . . . It seemed unbelievable that I, Wallis Warfield of Baltimore, Maryland, could be a part of this enchanted world." She was, she said, "Wallis in Wonderland."

But what was it about Wallis that so appealed to Edward? That was by no means so clear. She was not beautiful, nor was she very young, and Edward could certainly have found a woman who was both. Wallis herself, in her memoirs, said that she "could find no reason why this most glamorous of men should be seriously attracted to me." She attributed it to "my American independence of spirit, my directness, what I would like to think is a sense of humor and of fun, and well, my breezy curiosity about him and everything concerning him."

That was certainly a part of it. Her irreverent comments when they were introduced—whether in her own version or the duke's—would undoubtedly have been a breath of fresh air to a prince used to stuffy politeness.

Others found more titillating explanations. According to a 1935 report by British secret service agents, Wallis's first husband, during their stay in China, introduced her to Hong Kong's luxurious brothels, which were known as "singing houses." This led some later biographers to speculate that she'd learned the ancient art of *fang chung*. This consisted of a woman brushing her fingers across a man's nipples, stomach, thighs, and lastly—after a deliberate delay—genitals. Practitioners of fang chung learned the nerve centers of the body, providing them with further expertise on how to sexually excite a man.

And, according to some of the Duke's biographers, it took all of Wallis's seductive powers to arouse Edward. A playboy in public, in private he was anything but, according to various—and not always reliable—sources. At various times, he was rumored to be a latent homosexual, sterile (this based in part on Wallis's quip, when asked why she'd never had any children, that Edward wasn't "heir-conditioned"), or so inhibited that he was virtually incapable of having sex. (The last came from an admittedly bitter Thelma Furness.)

Wallis's sexuality also was the subject of much speculation. While some painted her as an expert in Eastern techniques, others described her as a lesbian or a virgin—the latter in spite of her two previous marriages.

The evidence for these exotic theories is certainly too slight to serve as a definitive explanation for the attraction of Wallis to Edward, or of Edward to Wallis. Besides, less sensational explanations are perfectly credible. Indeed, for all the talk about their sex lives, it seems likely that sex was *not* a particularly crucial part of their relationship. Wallis was open about how excited she was by Edward's lifestyle; it was an excitement that, if sexual, was only incidentally so. And Edward too was seeking more than sex. To many biographers, the salad incident Thelma witnessed indicated the true nature of their relationship: here were, not two passionate lovers, but a good-humored mother scolding her son for his bad manners.

Their letters to each other bear out that theirs was, in many ways, a mother-son relationship. His, often written in a baby-ish voice, plead for her approval; hers offer it, along with various admonishments to behave himself. Having been brought up by governesses and then shipped off to boarding schools, and having seen his parents mostly at official occasions, Edward desperately wanted a mother's love. He sought it in a succession of affairs with married women, first with Freda Dudley Ward, then with Thelma Furness, and finally and most satisfyingly, with Wallis Simpson.

Having finally found what he wanted, Edward was unwilling to give her up. Nor was he satisfied to keep Wallis as his mistress; he wanted to marry her. But by 1936, his situation was becoming untenable; what had been amusing gossip about the Prince of Wales was turning into a major scandal about the king of England. The opinion of his family and his ministers was increasingly that Wallis had to go.

Legally, there was nothing they could do about it. Edward was entitled to marry anyone he wanted—commoners, Americans, and divorcées included. After all, Henry VIII had created the Church of England just so he could marry Anne Boleyn, after the pope refused to let him divorce Catherine of Aragon. The only legal impediment to Edward's marriage to Wallis was that she was still married to Ernest Simpson, but divorce proceedings were already under way.

Edward's friends, among them Winston Churchill, urged him to be patient. Given time, Churchill was convinced, both the public and the royal family would come around. He suggested that Wallis withdraw for the moment, and that Edward put off any marriage plans until Wallis's popularity rose, perhaps through association with some charities.

Edward would hear none of this. He wanted to marry Wallis, and he wanted to do so right away. So when some advisers, possibly including Churchill, suggested a compromise that would allow him to do so, Edward jumped. The idea was that Edward and Wallis would have a "morganatic" marriage. This is a marriage in which a partner of lesser rank does not take on the higher rank that a marriage would normally bring. In other words, Edward would be king, but Wallis would not be queen, nor would their children inherit the throne. To Edward, it seemed an ideal solution, one that might mollify public opinion and his family, while still allowing him to marry Wallis. And Wallis, who realized that this was as close as she might get to being queen, was willing to go along.

The problem was that British law had no provisions for this type of marriage. There were some precedents in smaller European countries, but none in England. That meant that Edward, though he could legally marry Wallis without anyone's permission, required an act of Parliament for a morganatic marriage.

He also needed the approval of Canada and Australia which, though self-governing, still pledged allegiance to the crown.

Edward turned to his prime minister, Stanley Baldwin, telling him that Parliament and the dominions would have to choose between a morganatic marriage to Wallis or his abdication. In doing so, he sealed his fate, for having turned over the decision to others, he was bound by their decision. On December 2, 1936, Baldwin delivered their response. It amounted to an ultimatum: renounce Wallis or abdicate.

Why Edward boxed himself in has been a source of much speculation. Some have argued that Baldwin manipulated the king into asking for a decision from Parliament and the dominions. This explanation isn't fully satisfying. Baldwin was appalled by Edward's playboy image and by his sympathetic attitude, shared by many of his class, toward Nazism. But the prime minister's main concern was to avoid a constitutional crisis, and he repeatedly urged Edward to drop his plans to marry Wallis.

Others suspected that Edward intentionally brought on the crisis. According to this theory, Edward never really wanted to be king. Wallis provided him with an excuse for doing what he wanted to do anyway.

The most likely explanation for Edward's behavior is perhaps the most obvious. He wanted to be king, but not if it meant he couldn't have whatever else he wanted—which very much included Wallis. Eight days after Baldwin's ultimatum,

Edward abdicated. Six months after that, in a ceremony no other member of the royal family attended, Edward and Wallis were married.

❦— —❧

The Duke and the Duchess of Windsor, as they were now known, honeymooned in Venice, Italy, riding in gondolas and strolling through gardens like any other couple. Yet once the honeymoon was over, they faced a future that, though financially secure thanks to Edward's considerable personal fortune, was otherwise uncertain.

What exactly were an ex-king and his wife supposed to do with their lives?

Edward had in mind a return to something like his role as Prince of Wales, but his brother, now King George VI, made clear he wanted to keep Edward and any reminders of Edward's kingship, as far away from England as possible. "How do you think I liked taking on a rocking throne, and trying to make it steady again?" the new king wrote his brother. "It has not been a pleasant job, and it is not finished yet."

Edward's political views were also increasingly embarrassing, especially as the Nazi threat became clearer. The duke made matters much worse when he visited Germany in the fall of 1937. There he met with Hitler and was even photographed making a fascist salute. This was more than a public relations debacle; even granting that the duke could not have known the full danger of Nazism, he was playing into the hands of a government already at odds with that of his brother. In fact, there was a great deal of suspicion, after World War II began, that Hitler planned to conquer Britain and put Edward back on the throne as his puppet (presumably with Wallis as his queen).

The evidence of Edward's Nazi sympathies is overwhelming and damning, but it seems unlikely he would have consciously betrayed his country. More likely is that Edward went to Germany to bolster his ego. For all his rhetoric about his love mattering more than his crown, Edward undoubtedly missed some of the perquisites of kingship. In Germany, he was again treated like royalty and—equally important—so was Wallis.

In 1940, Churchill finally found a way to get the duke out of the way. He offered Edward the governorship of the Bahamas, a job which certainly had no significance in the midst of a world war. The duke and duchess reluctantly agreed, and they spent most of the remaining war years on the resort islands.

When writing to friends, Wallis would cross out "Government House, Nassau," on her letterhead, then write over it "Elba" or "St. Helena"—the islands to which Napoleon had been exiled.

After the war, their exile continued. The duke and duchess drifted from parties to golf courses and back again, living a life full of gaiety but without much more to it than that. Still, they remained faithful to each other.

By the 1960s, the hostility of the royal family had lessened, and the duke made periodic visits home, sometimes with the duchess accompanying him. Edward died in 1972, with Wallis at his side; Wallis, who became increasingly frail, lived on alone until 1986. Both are buried in the royal burial ground near Windsor Castle.

At no point in his life did Edward ever express any regrets about his decision to choose Wallis over the throne. A reporter once asked him if he sometimes wanted to give up his constant globe-trotting and settle down at home.

"Home," the duke responded, "is where the Duchess is."

12

Nancy and Ronald Reagan

"*M*y Darling First Lady," wrote Ronald Reagan in 1967, his first year as governor of California and his fifteenth year married to Nancy Reagan, "I'm looking at you as you lie here beside me . . . and wondering why everyone has only just discovered you are the First Lady. You've been the First—in fact the only—to me for fifteen years."

In 1985, by which time Nancy was the nation's First Lady, her husband declared publicly: "First Ladies aren't elected, and they don't receive a salary. They've mostly been private persons, forced to live public lives. And in my book, they've all been heroes. Abigail Adams helped invent America. Dolley Madison helped protect it. Eleanor Roosevelt was FDR's eyes and ears.

"And Nancy Reagan is my everything," he concluded.

Everything—in the eyes of their critics—included an undue influence over the president. The only First Lady more widely attacked on these grounds was Hillary Clinton. But the Clintons' disputes, political and personal, were out in the open.

Nancy Reagan, in contrast, operated behind the scenes. And with a husband who was always somewhat disengaged from the details of the presidency, and who by his second term may already have been suffering symptoms of Alzheimer's disease, the potential for manipulation was far greater than it was with Clinton.

Like Edith Wilson, who endured similar accusations, Nancy Reagan countered that she was only protecting her husband. "Ronnie tends only to think well of people," she wrote in her memoir. "While that's a fine quality in a friend, it can get you into trouble in politics."

Her husband agreed. In *his* memoir, he compared her to a bear rearing up on its hind legs when its mate or one of its cubs is in danger. "I know she's been accused of being a kind of 'shadow governor' or 'shadow President,'" he said. "Well, that's another myth. . . . she isn't trying to interfere with how I do my job, she just wants to keep me out of trouble."

"I was not," Nancy stressed, "the power behind the throne."

Perhaps not. But unlike Edith Wilson, who took a leading role only during the three months following her husband's stroke, Nancy Reagan was a force to be reckoned with long before her husband showed any signs of a disability.

Nancy Davis's courtship of Ronald Reagan was evidence both of her devotion to him and of her ability to manipulate him. In 1949, she was a moderately successful actress with a string of B movies to her credit. He was a star, though definitely on the downside of his acting career.

They met in the fall, by both their accounts, after she'd seen her name on a list of movie industry people supporting two Hollywood writers who had refused to cooperate with the House Un-American Activities Committee. As a lifelong conservative, she was upset to be listed alongside people she considered communist sympathizers. So she asked her friend Mervyn

LeRoy to call the president of the Screen Actors Guild to see if he could help.

The SAG president was Ronald Reagan.

Some have questioned the Reagans' story of their first meeting, claiming they'd already been introduced at a dinner party and that her fear of being tainted with communism was merely a ruse. In any case, whether from having met him in person or merely from seeing him on-screen, it was clear that Nancy Davis very badly wanted a date with Ronald Reagan.

Reagan was oblivious to this. After LeRoy called him, he looked into the matter and learned that it was a different Nancy Davis who was active in left-wing causes. Reagan reported this to LeRoy, who told Davis that if there was ever any confusion SAG would step in.

"That was reassuring," Nancy remembered, "but it wasn't exactly what I wanted to hear. So I put on a *very* unhappy face. 'I'm really worried,' I said. 'I'd feel a lot better if Mr. Reagan explained it to me himself.'"

LeRoy dutifully passed this on, and eventually Reagan called and asked her out to dinner. Technically, it was a blind date, but she admitted it was "blinder for him than for me."

The two began dating regularly, though not exclusively. Reagan was still recovering from his July 1949 divorce from Jane Wyman, who had wound up bored with what she considered his constant speechifying. "Don't ask Ronnie what time it is,"

Wyman once warned a friend, "because he will tell you how a watch is made."

Davis, in contrast, would listen to Reagan talk SAG—or national—politics with an adoring gaze. Her adoration was contagious.

"I did everything wrong, dating her off and on, continuing to volunteer for every Guild trip to New York—in short, doing everything which could have lost her," Reagan wrote. But eventually "Nancy moved into my heart and replaced an emptiness that I'd been trying to ignore for a long time."

Davis gave the romance another push in January 1952 when she told Reagan she was thinking about calling her agent about getting a role in a play in New York. Soon after, he proposed, and in March they were married.

Nancy Reagan had a very traditional attitude about marriage, and she planned to retire from acting to be a wife and mother. The Reagans' first child, Patti, was born eight months after their marriage, "a bit precipitously," Nancy conceded, "but very joyfully."

But Ron's acting career was on the skids. The type of old-fashioned movie that had made him a star was out of style, and so was he. So Nancy continued to work on and off until 1954, when he landed a job with General Electric.

Reagan hosted the company's weekly television show, but he also toured the country on behalf of GE. At first, he spoke mostly about the company's products, but gradually he pushed its politics as well. Eventually, he stopped talking about toasters and focused on the evils of big government.

It was during this period that Ronald Reagan, who had been a Roosevelt Democrat (as well as, given his SAG role, a strong unionist) moved decisively to the right. Many attributed this to his wife, who had always been a conservative, but it's at least as likely that the move had to do with his position as a corporate spokesman.

Reagan enjoyed the political speech making, but he missed his wife. "I'm sitting here on the 6th floor beside a phoney fireplace looking out at a grey wet sky and listening to a radio play music not intended for one person alone," he wrote her in March 1955.

By now, he was as completely in love with her as she was with him. His letter continued: "I wouldn't trade the way I feel for the loneliness of those days when one place was like another and it didn't matter how long I stayed away."

There was even more longing in a letter he wrote a month later: "Maybe we should build at the farm so we could surround the place with high barb wire and booby traps and shoot anyone who even suggests one of us go to the corner store without the other. How come you moved in on me like this? I'm all hollow without you and the 'hollow hurts.'"

And this, from a note sent in March 1956 for their fourth anniversary: "I should have married you so long ago this would be our Silver Anniversary. Anyway, I've had 25 years' happiness for each of the last 4."

❦—❧

On the career front, the next move for Reagan was, of course, to leave GE and fully enter politics. He served two terms as governor of California before carrying his conservative agenda to Washington.

For Nancy Reagan, the presidency brought with it the chance to restore to the White House the glamour that Jacqueline Kennedy had brought there. She devoted her first year to that— and it was an unmitigated disaster.

A month into office, on the same day the presidential edict counting ketchup as a vegetable in subsidized lunches went into effect, the First Lady announced the acquisition of $200,000 worth of new china for the White House. It was one thing for Jackie Kennedy, a Democrat, to make the White House chic. It was quite another for a Republican to do so amid cuts in social spending. With her expensive wardrobe and her plans to renovate the White House, Nancy Reagan came across, as Kitty Kelley put it, like "a Marie Antoinette windup doll."

Johnny Carson couldn't resist imagining the questions reporters might ask the First Lady at a press conference. "One was about Mrs. Reagan's religion, which we all know is Christian Dior, and her favorite junk food, which is caviar," he quipped. "Someone questioned her about foreign policy and whether or not she favored Red China. She said she did, but not with yellow tablecloths."

None of this was funny to the administration, which feared the First Lady would drag down the president's popularity. Wrote political analyst William Schneider: "It's hard to think of a First Lady who has been so damaging, but Mrs. Reagan . . . crystallizes an important criticism of this administration: its supposed bias toward the rich."

The First Lady's popularity, like the president's, improved drastically after he was shot in March 1981. Their courage and love for each other was manifest, and it moved Republicans and Democrats alike. The First Lady's "Just Say No" campaign against drugs also improved her image by demonstrating that she was interested in social problems as well as social climbing.

But the image of a loving, caring First Couple suffered a number of blows in the coming years, many at the hands of their children. In 1986, their daughter Patti published a novel, *Home Front*, about the daughter of an actor who becomes governor of California and then president of the United States. The novel was a bitter indictment of the Reagans' family life, even of the love between Patti's parents. It portrayed both as so devoted, first to each other and second to political success, that they had no interest at all in their own children.

This was especially embarrassing for a couple who had campaigned for traditional family values. In her memoir, Nancy argued, quite reasonably, that it was unfair to call them hypocrites just because their reality sometimes fell short of their ideals. But she admitted Patti's book hurt them, politically and certainly personally.

"What I wanted most in all the world was to be a good wife and mother," she wrote. "As things turned out, I guess I've been more successful at the first than at the second."

The revelations in *Home Front* were nothing compared to those of Donald Regan's 1988 book, *For The Record*. Regan, who was the president's chief of staff between 1985 and 1987, revealed that the president's schedule had for years been determined by astrologers.

Regan described lengthy phone conferences with the First Lady in which she passed on her astrologer's prognostications. "She had become such a factor in my work, and in the highest affairs of the nation," he wrote, "that at one point I kept a color-coded calendar on my desk (numerals highlighted in green ink for 'good' days, red for 'bad' days, yellow for 'iffy' days) as an aid to remember when it was propitious to move the President of the United States from one place to another, or schedule him to speak in public, or commence negotiations with a foreign power."

The First Lady didn't deny that astrology was a factor in determining the president's schedule, though she claimed— shades again of Edith Wilson—that the advice was limited to scheduling and never impinged on politics.

Regan also blamed Nancy for getting him fired. Far from the Marie Antoinette portrayed during her early reign as First Lady, she was now cast as Lady Macbeth, pushing her poison through her once-virtuous husband.

In his memoir, Ronald Reagan confirmed that his wife had urged him to fire Regan, though he emphasized, as always, that she was only interested in protecting him. Nancy's memoir also admitted she wanted Regan out, but downplayed her influence. "Believe me, if I were the dragon lady that he described in his book, he would have been out the door many months earlier," she wrote. "Did I talk to Ronnie about Don Regan? Absolutely. Did I pass on what I was hearing from White House officials and congressional leaders? Of course.

"But," she emphasized, "that doesn't mean Ronnie listened."

In fact, Regan might very well have survived the First Lady's animosity, had the Iran-contra scandal not plunged the administration into chaos late in 1986. "I'm not saying that Iran-contra was Don Regan's doing," she wrote. "But it did occur on his watch, and when it came out, he should have taken responsibility."

In February 1987, under pressure from congressional leaders as well as Nancy Reagan, Regan resigned.

Regan's accusations raised the question of whether the First Lady had too much power in general. There was a certain irony in this, especially since this was the same woman who had once been accused of caring about nothing but clothes and parties.

The charges were also sometimes contradictory. In the sixties, when Ronald Reagan first entered politics, liberals blamed her for his swing to the right. In the eighties, when the president backed away from his hard-line position with the Soviet Union, conservatives blamed her for his willingness to negotiate with Gorbachev.

The reality was that Nancy, as both she and her husband claimed, was generally not interested in pushing any particular policy. Her interest was in advancing and protecting her husband's interests; to further these ends, she looked to both the stars and, more sensibly, her own judgment. She wanted Regan fired because she thought he wasn't serving the president's interests, and she actively worked to get rid of him.

But the line between personal and political was a fine one, and she sometimes crossed it. Changing the president's chief of staff affected policy as well as personnel. Changing her husband's schedule to make sure it was in accord with the stars affected what he did as well as when. Occasionally, the private pressure she exerted was blatantly political, such as when she lobbied the president to pursue a diplomatic solution in Nicaragua or (more successfully) to soften his stance on the Soviet Union.

Her critics were outraged when she crossed this line. But, right or wrong, the criticism was naive: no one could expect a man and woman who so depended on each other—who so loved each other—never to talk politics.

Wrote the First Lady: "Did I ever give Ronnie advice? You bet I did. I'm the one who knows him best, and I was the only person in the White House who had absolutely no agenda of her own—except helping him."

The president agreed: "If you can't trust your wife to be honest with you, whom can you trust?"

He trusted her completely, and he continued to do so, even as Alzheimer's gradually robbed him of his mind. As he deteriorated, his biographer Edmund Morris wrote, she "made his 'long good-bye' as comforting as possible." At the time Morris wrote that, hers was the only face Ronald Reagan still recognized.

13

Grace Kelly
and Prince Rainier

*I*n the thirteenth century, not long after the Grimaldis gained control of Monaco, one member of their clan took a beautiful Flemish woman as his lover and then betrayed her. Soon after, the legend goes, she either turned herself into a witch or was turned into one by someone else. To avenge herself on her betrayer, she placed a curse upon him, saying that "never will a Grimaldi find true happiness in marriage."

Seven hundred years later, when another Grimaldi decided to get married, he couldn't be blamed if the curse made him hesitate. After all, as Prince Rainier III of Monaco knew all too well, his parents, his grandparents, and his great-grandparents had all been unhappily married.

Still, Rainier knew it was time to choose a bride. For, truth be told, his principality was looking a bit dowdy. Its casino and grand hotels lined the Mediterranean, but they weren't nearly as crowded as they'd been fifty or a hundred years before. Perhaps a marriage—to the right bride—could inject some glamour back into Monaco's international image.

And, curses aside, Rainier had a number of things going for him. There was a suitably grand, 800-year-old palace overlooking the Mediterranean with a yacht anchored below. True, Monaco covered less than a square mile. But the climate was perfect, there was virtually no crime, and Rainier was moderately good-looking and only thirty-one years old.

Indeed, Rainier was one of the world's most eligible bachelors. Let's face it: by the second half of the twentieth century, there simply weren't that many absolute rulers left for an ambitious princess-to-be to marry.

The princess, as Rainier saw things, had to meet a number of qualifications. She had to be fertile, of course, so she could bear an heir to the throne. She should be attractive and, like Rainier, Catholic. And, royal traditions being what they were, she'd need a sizable dowry, so she had to be rich as well. In short, Monaco needed a princess respectable enough to carry on the royal tradition, but glitzy enough to bring back the big spenders.

The prince's thoughts turned to Hollywood, perhaps because there were plenty of stars conveniently visiting the Cannes Film Festival, just an hour or so down the coast. The biggest of them all was Grace Kelly, who was there for a special screening of *The Country Girl*, for which she had just won the Academy Award for best actress. Grace had also starred in Alfred Hitchcock's *Dial M for Murder* and *Rear Window*, both released in 1954, and in Hitchcock's latest, *To Catch a Thief*, which had been filmed in and around Monaco. Her latest project, released in 1956, was *The Swan*, in which Grace played—you guessed it—a princess.

As fate would have it, Pierre Galante, the movie editor for *Paris Match* magazine, thought that a photo of Monaco's prince with Hollywood's reigning princess would make a good cover shot for its special issue on Cannes. Galante asked the prince if he'd be available for a photo shoot.

Rainier, somewhat to the editor's surprise, quickly agreed.

❧—❧

Grace was less enthusiastic. But she owed Galante a favor, so she arrived at the palace on May 6.

To her surprise, Grace liked the prince. He was attractive and funny and unpretentious, not the stuffy aristocrat she'd expected. After the photo shoot, Grace accepted the prince's offer to tour his private zoo, and she was further impressed when he put his arms through the bars of a tiger's cage and petted it as if it were a house cat.

On the way back to Cannes, Galante asked what she thought of the prince. "He is charming," she answered. When Grace returned to America, she wrote the prince a polite thank-you note.

Rainier was equally charmed. Grace was beautiful, rich, Catholic; she seemed to have all the right credentials, assuming she was fertile. The prince responded to her note with one of his own, and the two began a regular correspondence.

The timing was right for Grace, as well as for the prince and his principality. She'd had a number of affairs with her leading men, including Clark Gable and William Holden. But she had been raised as a Catholic, and she felt guilty about the relationships. Getting married would make her parents happy, and she believed it would make her happy too.

Grace also liked the idea of leaving Hollywood while she was still on top. She was a star, but she was never confident of her acting skills, and she worried about the roles she'd get as she aged.

In 1955, while she was making *High Society*, Gore Vidal asked her what would make her give up her career. "When I first came to Hollywood five years ago, my makeup call was at eight in the morning," she answered. "On this movie it's been put back to seven-thirty. Every day I see Joan Crawford, who's been in makeup since five, and Loretta Young, who's been there since four in the morning. I'll be goddamned if I'm going to stay in a business where I have to get up earlier and earlier and it takes longer and longer for me to get in front of a camera."

The question for both Grace and Rainier was how to move beyond the pen-pal stage. Again, fate intervened, this time in the form of a visit to the south of France by Edie and Russell Austin, who were friends and neighbors of the Kelly family. (Grace knew them as Aunt Edie and Uncle Russell, though they weren't blood relatives.)

Aunt Edie and Uncle Russell decided they wanted to attend the annual Red Cross Ball in Monaco, but it was sold out. Knowing Grace had met the prince, they decided to call the palace to see whether he could help. Rainier was glad to do so and even invited the couple to tea.

Several months later, the prince called the Austins to say he was coming to America in December. They invited him for lunch, and it was decided that they'd all then go over to the Kellys for Christmas dinner. So it was that, late on Christmas Day 1955, His Serene Highness arrived at the Kelly house in Philadelphia.

The dinner was a success. The prince hit it off, not just with Grace, but with her family. But there was still the delicate matter of Grace's fertility, and accounts differ as to how this was resolved. Some say Grace agreed to be tested (and passed). Others say she indignantly refused, partly because she didn't want the prince to know that she wasn't a virgin. One way or another the issue was resolved; Rainier himself later denied it was ever raised.

That left only the dowry to be settled, and it too turned out to be a sensitive matter. The money itself wasn't a problem: Grace was rich and so was her father, Jack Kelly, who had built a million-dollar construction business in Philadelphia. But Jack Kelly was enraged by the very idea of a dowry.

Recalled John Pochna, one of the lawyers involved in the negotiations: "Kelly reckoned his daughter was dowry enough for any goddamn suitor . . . Rainier might be 'My Lord Prince,' . . . but in the eyes of a right-thinking American he was just 'any damn broken-down prince who was head of a country over there that nobody knew anything about.'"

Somehow, this issue also was resolved. By some accounts, Jack Kelly agreed to pay a $2 million dowry, though both sides refused to give a figure.

The negotiations over, the marriage was set for spring. On April 4, 1956, Grace and her family set sail on the USS *Constitution*. Eight days later, Grace arrived in Monaco to wed her prince.

She was understandably nervous, since this was only the third time they'd met. But they both believed they were doing the right thing. "We happened to meet each other at a time when each of us was ready for marriage," Grace later said. "There comes a time in life when you have to choose."

The wedding went off without a hitch. Actually, it was three weddings that went off without a hitch, for in addition to a civil ceremony and a church ceremony, the couple held a separate ceremony for the benefit of MGM. The studio, in return for putting Grace's movie contract on indefinite hold, had obtained exclusive film rights to the wedding.

If Grace thought being a princess would be like a fairy tale, she quickly found otherwise. Naturally shy and speaking only a little French, Grace found herself alone much of the time that Rainier was at work. The servants were suspicious of the newcomer, as were many of the citizens of Monaco, who regarded her as the *American* princess. Royal protocol—she could never appear in public alone, for example—isolated her further.

Worse, Grace was surrounded by family intrigue. Rainier's sister, Princess Antoinette, had once plotted to overthrow the prince but had settled for the role of Monaco's First Lady. Now Grace had displaced her and she resented it, as did Rainier's mother, Princess Charlotte.

"Grace had great problems with Rainier's mother," recalled Grace's sister, Lizanne Kelly LeVine. "Cold wasn't the word for Charlotte's attitude towards Grace. . . . And Princess Antoinette wasn't any happier about the Prince marrying an American actress than Charlotte had been."

Rainier himself turned out to be something other than Prince Charming. Being absolute ruler over a country, however small, wasn't likely to train a man to consider a wife's feelings or to make the compromises marriage calls for. He expected to be king of the castle, both when it served as his office and when it served as his home. Grace later put it tactfully: "American women are outspoken, forthright, and honest and say what they think. And this shocks European men."

As if all that weren't enough for Grace to deal with, there was the constant barrage of press and photographers. As a movie star, Grace was used to being photographed, but she was not used to this complete loss of privacy. Much like Princess Diana twenty-five years later, she couldn't leave the palace without being hounded by paparazzi. Indeed, when Grace met Diana in

1981, the younger woman expressed her fears about the press. Grace could only say, "Don't worry, dear. It'll get worse."

Unlike Diana, however, Grace and Rainier actively courted publicity if they thought it would help Monaco's image. After all, that had been Rainier's plan from the start, and it succeeded beyond his dreams. The marriage brought a new aura of glamour to Monaco; more importantly, it again made Monaco a popular tourist destination.

Between 1955 and 1959, tourism doubled. This was partly because of growing European prosperity and the increase in tourism worldwide. But mostly it was because Grace put Monaco back on the map. People came for the casino and the beach and the oceanographic museum but, above all, they came because Monaco was the fairy-tale land where Grace Kelly had married her prince.

Their partnership in promoting Monaco wasn't the only bond between Grace and Rainier. The couple also shared a desire to be better parents than their own had been. Rainier's father and mother, who divorced, had been more concerned with battling each other than with raising their son, whom they quickly shipped off to boarding school. And Grace's parents, though loving, had been extremely strict and intimidating.

When Grace gave birth to Princess Caroline in 1957, Prince Albert in 1958, and finally Princess Stephanie in 1965, it was a cause for joy. For Caroline's birthday, the prince declared a national holiday: the casinos were closed, free champagne was served on the street, children were let out of school early, and the three prisoners in Monaco's jail were released.

Rainier and Grace were celebrating more than the continuity of the Grimaldi dynasty. Both would be happy and devoted parents.

To keep the children away from the press and to try to create some sort of normal family life, Rainier and Grace bought a farmhouse with sixty acres on the slopes of Mont Agel, which looked down on Monaco. Here they could be parents and children rather than princes and princesses, and though Rainier was still sufficiently chauvinistic to leave most of the child rearing to Grace, he was a caring and involved father.

And in loving the children together, Rainier and Grace grew closer to each other as well. Their marriage had been built on political and business considerations; Grace's sister even went so far as to call it, somewhat unfairly, an arranged marriage. But through the children, it deepened into one of respect and love. Rainier was still sometimes despotic, but they came to depend on and trust—and love—each other.

Still, Grace missed Hollywood. She'd chosen marriage over career, and she stood by that choice, but that didn't mean she never had any regrets. In 1962, she had a chance to return to moviemaking when Alfred Hitchcock asked her to star in *Marnie*.

Rainier, who had become a more sympathetic husband than he'd once been, encouraged Grace to go ahead. "There have been times when the princess has been a little melancholic, which I quite understand, about having performed a form of art very successfully, only to be cut away from it completely," he later said. "It was an idea that tickled her, and that she liked, and, quite frankly, I kind of pushed her into the solution."

What neither Grace nor Rainier anticipated was the uproar that followed their March 1962 announcement that she would appear in the film. The citizens of Monaco had finally come to accept Grace as *their* princess, and they considered it demeaning that she'd appear on-screen. What if the script called for her to *kiss* someone other than her husband? Local editorials screamed their disapproval.

MGM was also furious. The studio had been willing to put their contract with Grace on hold for the sake of her marriage, but they had no intention of letting her make a movie for someone else. They wrote an angry letter to Hitchcock.

To complicate matters further, the press speculated that Grace was doing the movie because the Grimaldis needed the money. Monaco was then in the midst of a dispute with the French government; the French were annoyed that Monaco was enticing not just tourists and gamblers but tax dodgers with its low tax rates. Rainier's showdown with President Charles de Gaulle actually had nothing to do with Grace accepting Hitchcock's offer, but the speculation added to the pressure on her to give up the movie.

In June, Grace backed out of the deal. Tippi Hedren ended up playing the title role in *Marnie*. (Rainier also bowed to the pressure from de Gaulle; Monaco continued to be a tax haven for other nationalities, but after 1962, French citizens there had to pay full French taxes.)

After the furor over *Marnie*, Grace looked elsewhere for creative outlets. During the seventies, she often spent much of the year in Paris, partly because her daughters went to school there, partly to escape the restrictions of palace life.

Starting in 1976, Grace began giving poetry recitals, a type of performance the people of Monaco deemed respectable. (It was at one such reading that she met Diana Spencer and comforted her about her loss of privacy.) And in the eighties, she began working toward the creation of a theater in Monaco.

Princess Grace did not, of course, live happily ever after. On September 13, 1982, while driving with Stephanie from their Mont Agel home down to the palace, Grace failed to make a hairpin turn and caromed off the mountainous road. Stephanie was not seriously hurt, but Grace died the next day.

After her death, the curse of the Grimaldis seemed to return. Princess Caroline was divorced and then widowed, Princess Stephanie divorced, and Prince Albert remained a bachelor.

But Rainier and Grace had remained committed until her death.

"I don't think that happiness—being happy—is a perpetual state that anyone can be in," Grace once admitted. "Life isn't that way. But I have a certain peace of mind . . . And my life here has given me many satisfactions in the last ten years." It was not, admittedly, an unconditional celebration of marriage—certainly not a description of the fairy-tale romance many imagined for her. But surely it was also not the witch's prophecy come true.

As Rainier once told an interviewer: "Yes, we beat the curse."

14

Camilla Parker Bowles
and Prince Charles

"There were three of us in this marriage," the Princess of Wales famously remarked in 1995, "so it was a bit crowded."

The princess's defenders seized upon her remark as a pithy explanation for the demise of the marriage between Prince Charles and Lady Diana Spencer. It was Charles's long-standing affair with Camilla Parker Bowles, they argued, that drove Diana to bulimia and suicide attempts. Diana, who loved her husband, simply couldn't cope with the knowledge that Charles loved somebody else all along.

Charles's defenders had a different spin. Charles had loved Camilla, they conceded, but he had given her up and made every effort to make his marriage work. But Diana's instability, as manifested in her bulimia and her obsessive suspicions about Camilla, rendered the marriage—in Charles's words—"irretrievably broken down." Only then, his supporters maintained, did Charles resume his relationship with Camilla.

So there were two versions of the battle of the Waleses, each put forward in countless articles and books. Both versions offered detailed analyses of the relationship between Charles and Diana, yet neither had much to say about the love between Camilla and Charles.

To Diana, Camilla was—understandably—nothing more than the other woman. And Charles, in his effort to counteract the vast public sympathy for Diana, tended to focus on Diana's problems rather than Camilla's virtues. Camilla herself was desperate to avoid the publicity that engulfed Charles and Diana, and she made no effort to emerge from the shadows of the palace.

The result was a remarkable paradox: perhaps the most widely publicized love story of our time, that of Charles and Camilla, also remained one of the most heavily shrouded.

◆— —◆

No one could have been better bred for the role of royal mistress than Camilla Shand, as she was known when she first met Charles in 1971 at Smith's Lawn, where he played polo. Camilla's great-grandmother, Alice Keppel, was the mistress of an earlier Prince of Wales, who later became King Edward VII. The two enjoyed a close physical and intellectual relationship that lasted from 1898 until Edward's death in 1912.

Camilla was fully aware of this history. According to one account, among the first things she said to Charles was: "My great-grandmother and your great-great-grandfather were lovers. So how about it?"

Charles was immediately attracted to Camilla's quick wit and directness. They also shared a love of equestrian sports, which is why they were both at Smith's Lawn. "She is about dogs and gun boots and a cozy life," said one friend.

Within months, Charles and Camilla were sleeping together.

Neither, however, raised the subject of marriage. Charles was only twenty-four and in no rush. Besides, he was then in the

Royal Navy, with an eight-month stint at sea ahead of him. In December 1972, he set sail for the Caribbean.

But Camilla, though only a year older than Charles, was ready to marry. With Charles away, she resumed an earlier relationship with Andrew Parker Bowles (who had once dated Charles's sister, Princess Anne). By the time Charles returned, Camilla was married.

"I suppose the feeling of emptiness will pass eventually," Charles wrote.

Over the next few years, the relationship between Charles and Camilla turned into a close friendship. She became his confidante, the person with whom he discussed the many women he dated, among them Princess Caroline of Monaco (the daughter of Prince Rainier and Grace Kelly) and Lady Sarah Spencer (Diana's older sister).

Andrew Parker Bowles, meanwhile, had a number of affairs, at least some of which Camilla knew about. She eventually decided that, though she wasn't prepared to leave him, she was ready for an affair of her own. In 1979, the friendship between Charles and Camilla again became a sexual relationship.

Even at this stage, the press rarely mentioned Camilla; its focus was on the younger and unmarried women who seemed much better candidates to become the Princess of Wales and the future queen of England. That was fine with Camilla and Charles, who enjoyed the relative privacy.

In 1980, Charles moved to Highgrove House, a 350-acre estate in Gloucestershire that he chose because it was only a few miles away from Camilla's house. Lightheartedly, Charles remarked to some schoolboys: "I hope you infants are enjoying your infancy as much as we adults are enjoying our adultery."

The comment didn't sit well with the royal family, even though nobody tied it to Camilla. The prince was no longer in his twenties, and the pressure to settle down (and produce an heir to the throne) was increasing. "You'd better get on with it, Charles," Prince Philip reportedly told his son, "or there won't be anyone left."

Charles pleaded for more time. In a BBC interview, he explained, "You've got to remember that when you marry, in my position, you are going to marry somebody who perhaps one day is going to become queen. You've got to choose somebody very carefully."

&— —&

Starting in 1980, of course, everyone's favorite candidate was Diana, whom Charles met at a party while she was sitting on a bale of hay. Like Charles, she professed to be interested in horses and country life; she came from a family that was suitably aristocratic; she was modest and pretty and funny.

Both families were pleased. The closest friend of the Queen Mother was Diana's grandmother, Lady Fermoy. Diana's step-grandmother, the romance novelist Barbara Cartland, said she didn't think Diana had ever had a boyfriend, adding: "She's as pure as one of my heroines."

The press screamed its approval. "Charles: Don't DIther," urged one headline. "To Di For," said another.

Even Camilla gave her stamp of approval. According to the version of the story pushed by the prince's defenders, Diana fooled everyone—Charles as well as Camilla. Once Camilla was convinced that Diana was the right woman for the prince and for the monarchy, she nobly stepped aside. Diana's supporters had a different version, of course; they believed Camilla okayed the marriage because she thought Diana was too naive to interfere with her own relationship with the prince.

Both versions seem unduly cynical. Most likely, Diana and Charles and Camilla all eventually found the pressure for the marriage irresistible. As Charles told a friend, "It is just a matter of taking an unusual plunge into some rather unknown circumstances that inevitably disturbs me but I expect it will be the right thing in the end."

Charles's proposal, in February 1981, was equally tentative. "Will you marry me?" he asked, and she quickly responded not only that she would but that she loved him very much.

"Whatever love is," Charles said.

Those three words would come back to haunt him, especially after he repeated them later that month when an interviewer asked the couple whether they were in love. It was about as soft a question, indeed as stupid a question, as anyone could ask, and Diana immediately answered, "Of course."

To his detractors, Charles's response was proof that he still loved Camilla and that his marriage never had a chance. That's not really fair to Charles. Before he proposed, Charles *did* end his affair (though not his friendship) with Camilla, and he *was* committed to making his marriage work. But for him, love was a complicated matter, involving public as well as private considerations. Moreover, he thought of himself as something of a philosopher, and he refused to give the press the simple sound bite the question obviously called for.

Two weeks before the wedding, Diana found more grounds for suspicion. She discovered a gold bracelet with the letters *G* and *F* intertwined. Gladys and Fred, she knew, were pet names Camilla and Charles had given each other. Diana confronted Charles, who admitted he planned to give the bracelet to Camilla, but argued it was a perfectly innocent and appropriate gesture of thanks for her friendship.

This led to a huge fight, after which Charles considered backing out of the wedding. He turned to his sister, Princess Anne, for advice, but she was in no mood to listen. She told him it was too late to change his mind, and she repeated Queen Victoria's advice to her daughter: "Just close your eyes and think of England."

If Diana thought the honeymoon cruise would leave Camilla behind, she quickly discovered otherwise. Two incidents inflamed her jealousy. First, while she and Charles were checking their appointment books, two photos of Camilla fluttered out of his. Then he appeared at dinner wearing a new pair of gold cuff links with intertwined *C*'s. He admitted the cuff links were a gift from Camilla, but again insisted it was a perfectly appropriate gift from an old friend.

And so it went through the early years of their marriage. Charles wanted the marriage to work, but he was completely bewildered by Diana's neediness. His royal upbringing left him aloof and restrained; it was not, as his detractors believed, that he didn't care, just that he didn't know how to show it. That made Diana all the more insecure and jealous, especially about Camilla.

There were, to be sure, periods of relative tranquility, especially after the births of William in 1982 and Harry in 1984. And in public, Diana was a brilliant addition to the royal family; her looks, her compassion, and her warmth endeared her to the public—especially because of the contrast to Charles's earnest but awkward philosophizing. But in private, Charles and Diana were increasingly estranged.

"I feel nowadays that I'm in a kind of cage. . . . I never thought it would end up like this," Charles wrote to a friend in 1986. "How could I have got it all so wrong?"

❧·—·❧

It was in 1986, Charles later admitted, that he gave up on his marriage, and that his friendship with Camilla turned back into an affair. Camilla welcomed the prince back, having realized by then that Andrew Parker Bowles was a chronic philanderer.

Leaving Diana in Kensington Palace, Charles now spent most of his spare time at Highgrove, from where he could easily visit Camilla. The staff at Camilla's home, noting his regular late-night visits, came to call Charles the "prince of darkness."

Around the same time, Diana also began a string of relationships with, among others, gin-company heir James Gilbey, royal riding instructor James Hewitt, and art dealer Oliver Hoare. Some of these may have remained platonic, but others were definitely not. So when Diana referred to the "three of us in this marriage," she was not being entirely candid; much of the time there were four.

This arrangement might have lasted; after all, plenty of couples have retained the facade of a marriage while living apart. Camilla and Andrew Parker Bowles both seemed perfectly satisfied, and Charles seemed resigned to the way things were.

Diana, however, was not. In 1991, she poured out her resentment to Andrew Morton, a reporter. Morton's 1992 book, *Diana: Her True Story*, didn't acknowledge Diana's direct cooperation, but still made clear how desperately unhappy the princess was. It revealed details of her bulimia, her suicide attempts, and her despair over Charles's affair, which she believed (wrongly) had gone on without interruption, even including the night before the wedding.

After the book was published—and serialized in the *London Times*, giving it more credibility than a tabloid publication—it was no longer possible to continue the masquerade. In December 1992, Prime Minister John Major officially informed the House of Commons that the couple had separated.

The reputation of Charles and Camilla, already at an all-time low after Morton's revelations, sank even further a month later with the publication of the "Camillagate" tapes. A phone conversation between Charles and Camilla had been recorded secretly in 1989, and now their sexual banter made international headlines. Most infamous was the following exchange:

CHARLES: The trouble is I need you several times a week.

CAMILLA: Mmmmm. So do I. I need you all the week, all the time.

CHARLES: Oh, God, I'll just live inside your trousers or something. It would be much easier!

CAMILLA: What are you going to turn into? A pair of knickers? Oh you're going to come back as a pair of knickers.

CHARLES: Or, God forbid, a Tampax, just my luck.

CAMILLA: You're a complete idiot! Oh, what a wonderful idea!

Ironically, the tapes in their entirety—and even in this silly exchange—reveal Charles and Camilla as a genuinely loving couple, sharing a sense of the absurd and still passionate about each other twenty years after their first meeting. The tapes were hugely embarrassing, of course, but no more so than it would be for any couple to have some of their most intimate conversations broadcast to the world.

The British public did not see it that way, however. By mid-1993, polls showed that more than half thought Charles was unfit to be king.

Andrew Parker Bowles also was not amused. It was one thing to have a quiet arrangement with his wife, but quite another to be described in the press as "the man who laid down his wife for his country." In January 1995, the Parker Bowleses were divorced. In August 1996, so were the Prince and Princess of Wales.

❦—◦❧

For the first time since 1973, Charles and Camilla no longer had to hide their love. After his divorce, Charles even expressed the hope that they might one day marry, though Diana's popularity made that unlikely.

In an effort to show the world that Camilla was something other than the other woman, the couple increased their public appearances, in spite of her desire to stay out of the limelight. This campaign seemed to be making some progress, especially after the prince hosted a fiftieth birthday party for Camilla in July 1997. "She was the first to arrive," reported the *Daily Mail*, "sweeping into Highgrove last night with all the confidence of a queen."

All that changed a month later when Diana was killed in a car crash in a Paris tunnel. Diana had always been more popular than Charles; after her death, she was so revered that it seemed almost sacrilegious to suggest anyone could take her place.

So Camilla and Charles's relationship again retreated into the palace's shadows. Gradually, the royal family came to accept her—in June 2000, for the first time since 1972, the queen spoke to Camilla. But there seemed little chance that she would become queen, or that she would emerge as a public figure. The love between Charles and Camilla can never again, of course, be a secret, but it seems destined to remain in the shadows.

Perhaps that's what they both prefer.

WRITERS AND ARTISTS

15

Gertrude Stein and Alice B. Toklas

*E*very Saturday night, the avant-garde would arrive at the apartment at 27, rue de Fleurus, in Paris. Before the First World War, they were mostly artists—Picasso, Matisse, Braque, Gris; after the war, there were more writers—Hemingway, Fitzgerald, Anderson, Ford.

Their hostess was Gertrude Stein, an American writer whose own writing was rarely read. She prided herself, it seemed, on making her work frustratingly abstract. Her descriptions were the literary equivalent of cubism; they approached the subject from many angles at once, creating what some saw as a new form of multidimensional portraiture and what others saw as merely an incomprehensible jumble.

Stein herself had no doubts about her work. "Einstein was the creative philosophic mind of the century," she explained, "and I have been the creative literary mind of the century."

Even those who found her writing unreadable couldn't deny her influence on the artists and writers who visited her apartment. "She had such a personality," Hemingway wrote, "that when she wished to win anyone over to her side she would not be resisted."

It was at the apartment on rue de Fleurus that, in the view of many cultural historians, modern art and literature were, if not born, then at least nurtured into maturity. So it's understandable that an occasional visitor to the apartment, eager to view the remarkable collection of Picassos and Matisses and angling for an audience with Gertrude, might not even notice that she did not live there alone. The apartment's other resident, Alice B. Toklas, was careful to stay in the background, cooking, serving, cleaning up.

In *The Autobiography of Alice B. Toklas* (which was actually written by Gertrude, not Alice), Gertrude had Alice describe her role this way: "The geniuses came and talked to Gertrude Stein and the wives sat with me."

Yet a regular visitor would know better than to run afoul of Alice. Those who did soon found themselves barred from Gertrude's salon. "Don't you come home with Hemingway on your arm," Alice told her, or at least so Gertrude reported in the autobiography. Sure enough, it wasn't long before Hemingway was no longer to be seen at the apartment.

Alice was Gertrude's cook, her housekeeper, her secretary, her editor, her publisher, and her lover. She was also, at least in some biographers' views, the power behind the modernist throne.

Gertrude grew up in Oakland, Alice in San Francisco. Both were Jewish, both came from well-off but by no means very rich families. But it took the San Francisco earthquake of 1906 to bring them together.

Gertrude had moved to Paris three years earlier, joining her brother Leo on the rue de Fleurus. Her brother Michael also lived in Paris with his wife, Sarah. After the earthquake,

Michael and Sarah returned to California to check out the damage to the family's property, and while they were in town, they met Alice. The Steins' talk of Paris captivated Alice, and a year later, she arrived on the rue de Fleurus. When they met, Gertrude was thirty-three, Alice thirty.

According to the autobiography, Alice heard bells ringing when she first met Gertrude. This was a sign, at least as Gertrude liked to tell the story, that Alice had encountered a genius. (Alice also heard bells when she first met Picasso and the philosopher Alfred North Whitehead.)

The bells were undoubtedly an example of Gertrude getting carried away by her own mythmaking. But there's no doubt that Alice genuinely believed Gertrude was a genius—and worthy of her complete devotion. Alice offered to type *The Making of Americans*, the long novel Gertrude was then working on. Every morning, she would arrive at the rue de Fleurus to type what Gertrude had written the night before. Soon she took over the housekeeping and cooking as well.

Gertrude, whose belief in her own importance never wavered, was delighted to find in Alice someone equally convinced. The two began taking long walks together, and Gertrude suggested Alice join the Steins for a summer in Tuscany. It was there, during the summer of 1908, that Gertrude proposed.

"Care for me," she pleaded. "I care for you in every possible way."

Alice agreed.

Even among the Parisian avant-garde, however, lesbianism was not then something to flaunt. So Gertrude and Alice took their vows in private, and it wasn't until early 1910 that Alice moved in with Gertrude and Leo.

It was in getting rid of Leo that Alice first demonstrated she was a force to be reckoned with. He had always ruled the roost: he was the one who originally set the tone for the Saturday night gatherings, lecturing to everyone about art, literature, and pretty much any other subject. Gertrude, the dutiful and adoring younger sister, had followed him from California to Cambridge to Baltimore to Paris, hanging on his every word.

But now there was Alice to reinforce Gertrude's conviction that it was *she*, not Leo, who was the genius in the family. "It is funny," Gertrude wrote in her usual meandering way, "this thing of being a genius, there is no reason for it there is no reason that it should be you and should not have been him, no reason at all that it should have been you . . ."

The first sign of sibling rivalry was a fight about Picasso. Leo admired the artist's technical skills, but he never liked cubism. Gertrude defended both Picasso and cubism wholeheartedly, especially since the latter mirrored her own literary experiments.

Gradually, Leo's criticism of Picasso extended to Gertrude's work as well. He called her writing "silly twaddle." This was more than Gertrude, egged on by Alice, could bear.

In the fall of 1913, Leo moved out. They split their art collection: he took the Renoirs and the Matisses; she kept the Cezannes and, of course, the Picassos. The apartment was now entirely Gertrude's—and Alice's.

After Leo left, brother and sister never spoke to each other again. Or, as Gertrude put it, "Little by little we never met again."

❧—❧

During World War I, Gertrude and Alice fled Paris, going first to Barcelona and then to the Mediterranean island of Majorca. Here Gertrude made their love the subject of a series of often-erotic poems, most famously the 1917 "Lifting Belly."

"I marvel at my baby. I marvel at her beauty I marvel at her perfection I marvel at her purity I marvel at her tenderness," she wrote. "I marvel at her industry I marvel at her humor I marvel at her intelligence I marvel at her rapidity I marvel at her brilliance I marvel at her sweetness I marvel at her delicacy, I marvel at her generosity, I marvel at her cow." (A cow, most Stein scholars believe, is an orgasm, though it's unclear how Gertrude came up with the term.)

Gertrude's love poems undoubtedly captivated Alice, just as her cubist word portraits intrigued the avant-garde. But both women found it increasingly frustrating, albeit understandable, that Gertrude's works reached only a very limited audience.

During the next decade, Gertrude's protégés rose to fame. Picasso and Matisse were already legends; soon Hemingway and Fitzgerald were too. Meanwhile, no one actually read Gertrude's books. She was famous, but most of her work remained unpublished or was privately published by Alice.

As the twenties turned into the thirties, Gertrude and Alice decided it was time for Gertrude to write a popular book. In 1932, in just six weeks, she did. The result was *The Autobiography of Alice B. Toklas*, a gossipy look at Gertrude's circle of artists and writers as seen through Alice's eyes.

The book was a bestseller. No one could believe the same woman who'd written sentences so convoluted that they were incomprehensible could turn around and write a memoir that was so much fun to read. So well did Gertrude mimic Alice's acerbic wit that many who knew them thought Alice really had written the book.

Perhaps Alice did contribute to the writing. In the autobiography, "Alice" says Gertrude urged her to try. "Just think . . . what a lot of money you would make," Gertrude supposedly said to Alice. "She then began to invent titles for my autobiography. My Life With The Great, Wives of Geniuses I Have Sat With, My Twenty-Five Years With Gertrude Stein."

Alice finally agreed to give it a try, but it didn't work out. "I am a pretty good housekeeper and a pretty good secretary and a pretty good editor and a pretty good vet for dogs and I have to do them all at once and I found it difficult to add being a pretty good author," Alice explained, in the book.

So Gertrude decided to write Alice's autobiography for her. The reaction was everything Gertrude and Alice had hoped for. For the first time, people were not just talking about Gertrude, but reading her book.

In 1934, a year after the book was published, Gertrude and Alice returned to America for the first time since 1903 and 1907, respectively. "I used to say that I would not go to America until I was a real lion a real celebrity at that time of course I did not really think I was going to be one," Gertrude later wrote, once again casting aside standard punctuation. "But now we were coming and I was going to be one."

It was a triumphant return home, as Gertrude lectured to admiring crowds across America. Alice, of course, worked behind the scenes, booking the lectures, making travel arrangements, and generally making sure things ran smoothly.

Not surprisingly, though, many of Gertrude's friends were none too pleased with how they came across in the autobiography. Matisse was angry about the description of his wife that compared her to a horse. Picasso's wife was upset by the discussion of her husband's former mistress, and it was two years after the book's publication before Picasso and Gertrude became friends again. And Leo, though surprised that his sister had written something that made sense, couldn't help but add: "But God what a liar she is!"

The unusual form of autobiography—Gertrude as writer, but Alice as narrator—may have enabled Gertrude to express her opinions on her circle more freely than otherwise. Of Hemingway, for example, Gertrude-as-Alice wrote that he was "fragile" and "yellow," characterizations that she had to know would offend the macho writer.

Would Gertrude have let such a damning description come out of her own mouth? Perhaps. The two had argued previously, in part because Gertrude felt Hemingway was homophobic. But no doubt it was easier for Gertrude to have the insults come out of Alice's mouth. And, indeed, the real Alice, who had always been jealous of Hemingway's friendship with Gertrude, would certainly have said much worse.

Hemingway eventually took his revenge with a vicious description of Gertrude and Alice that appeared in his own memoirs years later. More immediately, he sent Gertrude a copy of his latest book, *Death in the Afternoon*. The inscription, a play on Gertrude's famous line, "A rose is a rose is a rose," read: "A bitch is a bitch is a bitch. From her pal Ernest Hemingway."

⟵•——•⟶

The 1934–1935 tour of America was their last visit home. Gertrude and Alice lived the rest of their lives in France.

They remained there even during World War II—an extraordinarily dangerous decision in light of the fact that both were Jewish and the country was occupied by Nazi troops. They survived partly by passing themselves off as Frenchwomen and partly with the help of friends high up in the French government. To make ends meet, they sold one of the Cezanne paintings Gertrude and Leo had bought more than thirty years earlier.

In July 1946, Gertrude died from colon cancer and was buried in Paris. Alice lived another twenty-one years, supervising the posthumous publication of many of Gertrude's books and, as always, looking out for Gertrude's interests.

Alice also wrote three books of her own—two cookbooks and a memoir, this one really by her. *The Alice B. Toklas Cookbook*, published in 1954, was an unusual combination of recipes and reminiscences. Among the former was one called Hashish Fudge. Some readers felt the hash might offer a new explanation for Gertrude's more inscrutable writings, and Alice's friend, Thornton Wilder, complimented her on "the publicity stunt of the year." Alice was furious about the whole brouhaha.

Alice's memoir, *What is Remembered*, was published in the spring of 1963. Like *The Autobiography of Alice B. Toklas*, it focused mostly on Gertrude Stein. *Time* magazine called it the "book of a woman who all her life has looked in a mirror and seen someone else."

After Alice died in March 1967, she was buried—according to her careful instructions—in the same tomb as Gertrude. Her name, date of birth, and date of death appear on the same stone as Gertrude's, but on the back.

"Even in death," wrote her biographer Diana Souhami, "she did not want to encroach on Gertrude's fame and reputation. "The back of the headstone is not visible from the cemetery path and only those who know will step over other graves and find proof, engraved in gold, that Alice is there too."

But there she was, right behind Gertrude, all along.

16

Georgia O'Keeffe and Alfred Stieglitz

*O*n New Year's Day 1916, Alfred Stieglitz was sitting alone in the gallery known as 291 for its address on New York's Fifth Avenue. It was here that Stieglitz— perhaps the most influential art dealer in the country—had introduced Americans to the work of Cezanne, Braque, Matisse, and other European modernists; here that Picasso and Brancusi had had their first one-man exhibitions. Stieglitz was himself a famous artist whose photographs of snow and rain had done much to bring about the recognition of photography as an art form. At fifty-two, he was clearly established as one of the most important figures in art history.

None of this intimidated Anita Pollitzer, a young art student who walked right up to Stieglitz that New Year's Day. Pollitzer had under her arm some abstract charcoal drawings by her friend Georgia O'Keeffe, a twenty-eight-year-old art teacher who had worked at various elementary and high schools and was now at an obscure college in Canyon, Texas.

O'Keeffe had sent the drawings to get her friend's opinion, not to show to anyone else. But Pollitzer, sensing they were something special, took them to 291 and spread them on the floor in front of Stieglitz.

He looked at the drawings earnestly and silently for a long while, Pollitzer later recalled. Then he exclaimed, "Finally, a woman on paper!"

It was, undeniably, a sexist remark, implying that no other woman had ever successfully represented her sexuality (or her gender) in the art world. But it was also a profoundly prophetic remark, since Alfred Stieglitz already recognized that Georgia O'Keeffe could become the most famous woman artist in history. He kept the drawings and hung them on the walls of 291.

O'Keeffe was thrilled that the dealer liked her drawings, but furious that he had put her very private feelings on public display. After arriving in New York, she stormed into 291, introduced herself, and demanded that he take them down.

"You have no more right to withhold these pictures," he responded, "than to withdraw a child from the world."

His response flattered and calmed her, and they began talking. What eventually emerged was a love and marriage that was also one of the most productive and intriguing artistic collaborations of all time.

     ❧•—•❧

She was still teaching in Texas. He was still living with his wife, Emmeline, albeit in a loveless marriage. So O'Keeffe and Stieglitz came to know each other through their letters and through their work.

In the spring of 1917, just over a year after he'd first hung some of O'Keeffe's drawings in his gallery, Stieglitz presented a one-woman show. In May, she arrived in New York, but the show had already closed. In a grand gesture, Stieglitz rehung the exhibition for an audience of one—O'Keeffe.

With Georgia spending some time in New York, Alfred fell in love with the woman as well as her art. He introduced her to members of his circle, including his young protégé, Paul Strand, who would eventually take his place alongside Alfred as one of the country's greatest photographers. Strand too fell for Georgia.

After she returned to her job in Texas, the two men would sit around talking about her, though neither would admit he loved her. They became especially agitated after hearing about an incident during which Georgia's roommate, Leah Harris, used a pistol to chase off an intruder. Texas was not the place to nurture O'Keeffe's talent, Stieglitz and Strand agreed. And it was clearly too dangerous for young women on their own.

So Stieglitz dispatched the younger man to bring her back to New York. O'Keeffe, who was ready to give up teaching and concentrate on her art, agreed. In June 1918, she moved into a 59th Street studio just vacated by Alfred's niece.

A few weeks later, he began photographing her there, something he continued to do almost until his death. Over the next twenty years, Alfred would take hundreds of photos of Georgia, and they remain among his best work. Together, they form perhaps the most remarkable composite portrait of all time. She appears both nude and clothed, earthy and dreamy, sexual and distant; she is as enigmatic as the Mona Lisa.

One day in July 1918, Alfred decided to photograph Georgia at his Madison Avenue home instead of the studio. Emmeline arrived home during the shoot and found her husband with Georgia, who was nude. She threw the photographer and his model out of the house.

Alfred maintained that he and Georgia were completely innocent, that what they were engaged in was art and nothing else. "We weren't doing anything," he insisted then and later.

But Emmeline knew better. Exactly when Alfred and Georgia began sleeping together is impossible to document, but the photographs make clear his desire for her. Indeed, Alfred didn't deny the connection between his passion and his art. "When I make a photograph, I make love," he said—and that's what he was doing that July afternoon, even if he and Georgia weren't having sex.

Right after Emmeline threw him out, Alfred moved into the studio with Georgia.

In 1921, when Stieglitz's photographs of O'Keeffe were first exhibited, the explicit sexuality created a scandal. One critic, Lewis Mumford, called the portrait "the exact equivalent of the report of the lover's hand, exploring the body of his beloved."

But if Emmeline was right to see more than art at work, Alfred was certainly right to describe it as art. Indeed, it was great art, especially because it so well captured the complexity of Georgia and her relationship with Alfred.

Moreover, O'Keeffe was clearly Stieglitz's collaborator as well as his model. Like Stieglitz, she was fully aware of how the camera saw her and of the image she projected on film. In helping him to create his masterpiece, she advanced his art and his reputation just as surely as he did hers when he hung her drawings on the walls of 291.

❦—❧

In March 1924, O'Keeffe and Stieglitz held their first joint exhibition, which he arranged at the Anderson Galleries in New York. The show featured sixty-one of his prints and fifty-one of her paintings. In December, the collaboration became legal, when—three months after Emmeline granted him a divorce—Alfred and Georgia were married.

It was a remarkably productive union for both. She reinvigorated his photography, giving him a new subject that he continued to mine with great success. His work also inspired her; its influence could be seen almost immediately in the 1916 watercolor *Train at Night in the Desert*, which was based on one of his photographs. More importantly, he gave her the confidence to experiment with new styles and subjects, while using his promotional savvy to help make her a household name.

On the other hand, Stieglitz's support—though always wholehearted—was not always appreciated. For one thing, O'Keeffe was annoyed by his insistence on the sexual and feminine nature of her art. From the time he first announced that here was, finally, "a woman on paper"—he focused on these elements in her work. She became more impatient when critics followed Stieglitz's lead, finding sexual imagery in almost all her paintings, especially her famous paintings of flowers.

Undeniably, some of her paintings *were* sexually charged, but O'Keeffe rightly felt that she was being painted into a corner not entirely of her own making, and that Stieglitz was denying all other aspects of her art. It didn't help matters any that she had first become famous through the sexually explicit photos he took of her.

More mundane problems in their relationship also surfaced as the twenties progressed. Alfred hated to leave New York; Georgia yearned to travel. Alfred loved to talk about his philosophy of art; Georgia was more intuitive and preferred creating art to talking about it. And the twenty-four-year gap in their ages became harder to overlook as Alfred's various kidney and heart problems seemed to demand that she act as his nurse as well as his muse.

By the end of the decade, O'Keeffe felt trapped in New York, artistically and personally. She recalled with longing her feelings of freedom and discovery when she'd lived in Texas and visited New Mexico and Colorado. She wanted to move west, even if it meant leaving Stieglitz behind.

◆•— •▶

Reluctantly, Stieglitz agreed that O'Keeffe should visit New Mexico without him. In 1929, she spent the months of April through August in Taos, and she was ecstatic. Both her spirits and her work revived.

"You know I never feel at home in the East like I do out here," she wrote home that summer. The sunsets and skeletons of the

Southwest became her new subjects, inspiring many of her greatest works.

Thus began a new phase in their love. For the next twenty years, Georgia would split each year between New York and New Mexico. New York was for her husband, New Mexico for herself—and her art.

Gradually, Alfred and Georgia came to depend less on each other. Alfred turned to Dorothy Norman, a wealthy sponsor of his new gallery, who became his lover as well as, tellingly, his model. Georgia was rumored to have had several relationships during the ensuing years, with both men and women. (The latter, by some accounts, included Beck Strand, Paul's wife.)

But though they spent more time apart and each took other lovers, neither Alfred nor Georgia considered a permanent split. They wrote each other daily; over the course of their life together, they exchanged more than eighteen hundred letters and telegrams.

For Alfred, six months with Georgia was better than nothing at all. And gradually he, for whom art was always all-important, came to realize that her time away from him was essential to her art.

In June 1946, just before Georgia flew to New Mexico, Alfred wrote her a letter so that she would get it on her arrival. "It is hard for me to realize that within a few hours you will have left," he said. "But there is no choice. You need what 'Your Place' will give you. Yes you need that sorely. And I'll be with you . . . And you'll be with me here."

When others asked him about Georgia's absences, he would often respond: "How can I be jealous of a place?"

For O'Keeffe, who treasured her independence, Stieglitz was now an obligation, but he was never just that. She knew what she owed him for promoting her work. But she also knew that he had been, and to some extent continued to be, an inspiration to her.

"There is something about being with Stieglitz that makes up for landscape," she wrote Beck Strand after returning to New York in September 1930. Two years later, she wrote her friend Russell Vernon Hunter, "I am divided between my man and a life with him—and something of the outdoors . . . that is in my blood."

Eight years later, she wrote to the critic, Henry McBride: "Aside from my fondness for him personally I feel that he has been very important to something that has made my world for me—I like it that I can make him feel that I have hold of his hand to steady him as he goes on."

In July 1946, Stieglitz died of a massive stroke. O'Keeffe continued to spend a part of the next two years in New York, mostly to take care of dispersing his huge art collection. In 1949, having completed that task, she moved to New Mexico, where she lived until her death in 1986.

Still, Stieglitz's memory remained a strong force in her life. In 1976, she wrote: "I could see his strengths and weaknesses. I put up with what seemed to me a good deal of contradictory nonsense because of what seemed clear and bright and wonderful."

In her final years, partially blind, O'Keeffe came to depend on a young artist named Juan Hamilton, who managed her household and taught her pottery. Hamilton was born in 1946, the year Stieglitz died.

It's unlikely, therefore, that many people thought to put a photo of Hamilton next to one of Stieglitz at the same age. But those who did couldn't help but notice a striking resemblance between Hamilton and a young Alfred Stieglitz.

17

Scott and Zelda Fitzgerald

"*I* hate a room without an open suitcase in it," Zelda Fitzgerald once remarked. "It seems so permanent."

There was little permanence in the life she and her husband, F. Scott Fitzgerald, shared in the early twenties. The couple flitted from party to party, from New York to Paris, embodying the Jazz Age. Indeed, it was Scott who named the age in his 1920 novel, *This Side of Paradise*. Like his characters, Scott and Zelda were young and beautiful and, as the book sold, rich and famous. And they did not hesitate to celebrate all that.

Everyone invited them to parties and, more often than not, they went. Dorothy Parker remembered a taxi pulling up—with Zelda on the hood and Scott on the roof. She jumped into the fountain at Union Square and he, not to be outdone, jumped into the one in front of the Plaza Hotel. They were thrown out of the Biltmore Hotel for disturbing other guests, so they moved on to the Commodore—where they proceeded to spin around in the revolving doors for half an hour.

"I was in love with a whirlwind," he said. And she was in love with him. When they danced, she recalled, "There seemed to be some heavenly support beneath his shoulder blades that lifted his feet from the ground . . . as if he secretly enjoyed the ability to fly but was walking as a compromise to convention."

Scott remembered the early twenties as a time "when we drank wood alcohol and every day in every way grew better and better, and it seemed only a question of a few years before the older people would step aside and let the world be run by those who saw things as they were."

But they did not grow better and better. Instead, the stock market crashed . . . and so did Scott and Zelda.

◆•——•◆

Zelda Sayre was the life of the party well before she met Scott. The daughter of a judge in Montgomery, Alabama, Zelda reveled in shocking her conservative family and neighbors. Her reputation reached as far as Auburn University, where her suitors named their fraternity Zeta Sigma—in honor of her initials.

"When she came into a ballroom," one friend recalled, "all the other girls would want to go home because they knew the boys were going to be concentrating on Zelda."

It was at one such dance in July 1918 that she met Scott, who was a first lieutenant in the army and was stationed nearby. He, too, loved drinking, parties, and wild behavior. The two were soon an item. That summer they slept together, and when Scott left Alabama in the fall, he was in love.

Zelda was by no means as sure about him. For one thing, Scott's prospects were not promising. So far, his short stories as well as his novel had yielded only rejection letters. In New York, Scott landed a job working for an advertising agency where the best line he came up with—for a laundry in Iowa—was "We keep you clean in Muscatine." It did not seem to herald a brilliant literary career.

Zelda wrote Scott: "There's nothing in all the world I want but you—and your precious love. All the material things are nothing." But then she added: "I'd just hate to live a sordid, colorless existence, because you'd soon love me less."

So Zelda continued to see other men, while Scott courted her from afar. In the spring of 1919, he proposed a visit. She said she'd be delighted to see him—except for the week of June 13, when she was going to Georgia Tech for a graduation party where she planned, she explained, "to try my hand in new fields."

Scott tried to respond in kind by making her jealous of a woman he'd met in New York, but there was no way to beat Zelda at her game. "If she's good-looking, and you want to one bit," she responded, "I know you could and love me just the same."

This was hardly the reassurance Scott sought—especially since it implied that whatever love Zelda had for him didn't preclude her seeing other men.

Things got worse when Scott arrived in Atlanta to meet her and found he was one of five men there for that purpose. When Zelda refused to make any commitment to him, he stormed back to New York, boarding a first-class car to show her what she was missing (and then sneaking into coach, which was all he could actually afford).

"I used to wonder why they locked princesses in towers," Scott wrote on his return to New York. Clearly he felt that someone ought to lock up his.

Then Scott's situation suddenly improved. Magazines started buying his stories, and in September, Maxwell Perkins, an editor at Scribner's, informed him the company would publish *This Side of Paradise*.

On March 26, 1920, Scribner's released the book, and Scott was on his way to fame and fortune. Eight days later, he and Zelda were married in the rectory of St. Patrick's Cathedral in New York.

❦— —❧

Scott followed up *This Side of Paradise* with *The Beautiful and Damned* in 1922 and *The Great Gatsby* in 1925. Both sold moderately well, but not well enough to cover the couple's lifestyle. Scott was forced to churn out some second-rate stories for magazines, just for the cash, and then try an unsuccessful stint as a Hollywood screenwriter.

Max Perkins blamed Zelda: "Scott was extravagant, but not like her," he said. "Money went through her fingers like water; she wanted everything."

Zelda tried to make a joke of her spending. In a tongue-in-cheek review of *The Beautiful and Damned* in the *New York Tribune*, she urged people to get the book for the following "aesthetic" reasons: "First, because I know where there is the cutest cloth-of-gold dress for only three hundred dollars in a store on Forty-second Street, and also, if enough people buy it, where there is a platinum ring with a complete circlet."

But as the twenties progressed, people weren't laughing as hard as they once had. The Fitzgeralds' escapades began to seem less funny and more malevolent. At a restaurant in Cannes, the couple threatened to push the waiters off a cliff. Outside a casino, an old lady offered them a tray of nuts and candies, and Scott kicked the tray into the street. In Hollywood, when they weren't invited to Sam Goldwyn's party, they showed up anyway, got down on their hands and knees, and barked loudly until they were let in.

Most of the time, it was alcohol that turned what began as a silly prank into something boorish or worse. At their own parties, there was always plenty to drink and not much else. The novelist John Dos Passos recalled visiting them in Delaware (where they'd retreated, supposedly so Scott could get some work done). "Those delirious parties of theirs; one dreaded going," he said. "Dinner was never served . . . I remember going into Wilmington . . . trying to find a sandwich."

Zelda's flirtations began to seem less innocent too. During the summer of 1924, while Scott was writing *Gatsby* on the French Riviera, Zelda became involved with a young French flyer named Edouard Jozan. The two were seen together on the beach and dancing at the casino. The affair was brief, and some biographers have doubts about whether Zelda and Jozan slept together, but it shook the marriage nonetheless.

In 1927, in what he admitted was a "sort of revenge," Scott had a brief affair with an actress named Lois Moran. He defended the relationship to Zelda by telling her that at least Moran was doing something with her life.

Scott's words hurt, all the more because they echoed what others were saying. Ring Lardner said, "Mr. Fitzgerald is a novelist and Mrs. Fitzgerald is a novelty." Perkins thought of her as nothing but a drain on Scott's pocketbook and genius. And Ernest Hemingway blamed her too. "If he could write a book as fine as *The Great Gatsby* I was sure that he could write an even better one," he said. "I did not know Zelda yet, and so I did not know the terrible odds that were against him."

Zelda didn't think much of Hemingway either. She described the subject of his novel *The Sun Also Rises* as "bullfighting, bullslinging, and bullshit." But it wasn't just Hemingway or Perkins or Lardner; the consensus of those who knew them was that Zelda's drinking and partying were ruining Scott.

Most painful of all, Zelda could see some truth in the charges. Her dreams had come true; she was more glamorous than she could possibly have hoped for back in Alabama. Yet what did she have to show for it? What had she accomplished? Nothing.

Zelda decided that she too would become a writer.

The decision did not come out of the blue. In her review of *The Beautiful and Damned*, Zelda had written—jokingly, but tellingly—that on one page she "recognized a portion of an old diary of mine which mysteriously disappeared shortly after my marriage, and also scraps of letters which, though considerably edited, sound to me vaguely familiar."

She went on: "Mr. Fitzgerald—I believe that is how he spells his name—seems to believe that plagiarism starts at home."

Clearly Scott's fiction drew not just on their life together, but on Zelda's diaries and letters. Zelda had also written a few short stories on her own, though they were published under Scott's name since that brought more money.

Still, it seemed impossible to compete with Scott as a writer, and she couldn't bear to be overshadowed by him. So, in the summer of 1928, Zelda decided instead to devote herself to ballet. She threw herself into dance—body and soul. She took lessons and danced continually, in front of a mirror when she was alone and in front of guests when she wasn't.

Years later, in her autobiographical novel, *Save Me The Waltz*, Zelda described her obsession with ballet. "She would drive the devils that had driven her," she wrote. "She would achieve that peace which she imagined went only in surety of one's self . . . she would be able, through the medium of the dance, to command her emotions . . . She drove herself mercilessly."

Zelda's dedication, alas, was not enough. She was already twenty-six when she started dancing seriously, far too old to make it to the top ranks of ballet. "Zelda was awkward, her legs were too muscular, there was something about her intensity when she danced that made her look grotesque," said a sympathetic friend.

"She had a compulsion to compete with me," Scott said. "She could not as a writer, so she decided to be a famous ballerina. . . .

But it was too late for her. And when she realized this, instead of accepting the fact and bending with it, she broke."

Her breakdown first manifested itself clearly while they were driving to Paris from the Riviera in September 1929. Zelda suddenly turned the steering wheel and had to be restrained from plummeting over a cliff. In April 1930, she collapsed completely and had to be hospitalized in Paris.

Her doctors said she was suffering from either schizophrenia or dementia. She was often incoherent, but her description of her illness was vivid: "For months I have been living in vaporous places peopled with one-dimensional figures and tremulous buildings until I can no longer tell an optical illusion from a reality."

Meanwhile, Scott's life was also veering out of control. He had to pay for Zelda's hospitalization at just the time when sales of his books and stories were slowing down. After the stock market crashed, Americans were no longer so interested in reading about the rich and glamorous.

Scott began work on *Tender Is the Night*, an ambitious novel that would probe the causes of Zelda's madness through the story of a successful psychiatrist who marries a beautiful but troubled patient. The main character, Dick Diver, ends up losing both his wife and his career, a fate Scott certainly feared would be his own.

✦— —✦

Courageously, Zelda attempted to fight her way out of her madness. Realizing she could never be a famous ballerina, she returned to writing. In 1932, while she was in a hospital in Baltimore, she wrote *Save Me The Waltz*, her fictionalized account of her relationship with Scott and her breakdown.

In this version of their story, the heroine is named Alabama and her husband is David Knight. The names conjure up not only Zelda's home state, but Scott's characterization of her, during their courtship, as the princess in the tower with him playing the role of her knight. The novel tells the story of Alabama's marriage to Knight, a famous painter, her affair with a French aviator, her desire to become a ballet dancer, and her illness (which is physical and not mental in the book).

After finishing the manuscript, Zelda wrote Scott: "You will like it. It is distinctly Ecole Fitzgerald." Without telling him, she then sent the manuscript directly to Max Perkins at Scribner's.

When Scott read the manuscript, he was furious. It was one thing for him to draw on their lives together for his books, quite another for Zelda to do the same. Her book would preempt what he'd written so far of *Tender Is the Night*. To secretly send it to *his* publisher was even more of a betrayal. He wrote her psychiatrist: "This mixture of fact and fiction is simply calculated to ruin us both or what is left of us and I can't let it stand."

It all came to a head in May 1933, when Scott and Zelda confronted each other in person, with her doctor as mediator.

"You are a third-rate writer and a third-rate ballet dancer," Scott told Zelda, hitting her where it hurt. "I am a professional writer, with a huge following."

"It seems to me you are making a rather violent attack on a third-rate talent then," she retorted.

Then she struck back where it would hurt him most. She pointed out that he hadn't produced a novel since *Gatsby* eight years before. If he'd concentrate on his own work, he wouldn't be "so miserable and suspicious and mean towards everybody else."

Back and forth they went, with Scott claiming that, as the professional writer, the material of their lives belonged to him, and Zelda insisting that she wanted to be an artist in her own right. Finally, the psychiatrist intervened. He asked Zelda the decidedly unfeminist question: would she rather have her marriage or her writing?

"What is our marriage anyway?" she responded. "It has been nothing but a long battle ever since I can remember."

"I don't know about that," said Scott. "We were about the most envied couple in about 1921 in America."

"I guess," said Zelda. "We were awfully good showmen."

✦— —✦

Zelda agreed to let Scott edit her book, and he took out the parts he felt would undercut his book or reputation. Scribner's published *Save Me The Waltz* in October 1932 to poor reviews and poor sales. Zelda continued to write, but she now devoted most of her artistic energies to painting, where she again showed some talent but had no great success.

Zelda never truly recovered from her mental illness, moving in and out of various institutions until her death in 1948. Scott's reputation and sales also never recovered until well after his death in 1940.

But strangely, in spite of her madness and his drinking, in spite of their fighting and frustration, they remained in love. After Zelda was more or less permanently institutionalized, Scott began a lengthy relationship with Sheilah Graham, a Hollywood gossip columnist. But he remained loyal to Zelda, paying for her hospitalization and visiting her to remind her of better times. In 1935, he wrote a poem that began: "Do you remember, before keys turned in the locks/When life was a closeup, and not an occasional letter/That I hated to swim naked from the rocks/While you liked absolutely nothing better?"

Zelda, even in her madness, reached out to Scott. In one letter from the hospital, she wrote him: "I am sorry . . . that there should be nothing to greet you but an empty shell. . . . I love you anyway—even if there isn't any me or any love or even any life."

And in her lucid moments, Zelda too remembered better times. In another letter, again harking back to their courtship, she described herself to Scott as "a lady who was once . . . a princess in a high white tower . . . who is waiting once more for her royal darling."

18

Lee Krasner and
Jackson Pollock

*T*oward the end of 1941, the art impresario John Graham organized a show, American and French Paintings, for the McMillen Gallery on New York's 55th Street. Along with the French masters, Graham approached three Americans—Willem de Kooning, Jackson Pollock, and Lee Krasner—whom he placed at the forefront of a new movement later called abstract expressionism.

Krasner, at that point, was probably the best known of the three. She was familiar with all the Europeans in the show, of course, and she knew about Willem de Kooning as well. But she'd never heard of Jackson Pollock.

She prided herself on her art world connections. "I was in a rage at myself, simply furious because here was a name that I hadn't heard of," she recalled. "All the more furious because he was living on Eighth Street and I was on Ninth."

Not one to dither, Krasner went over and knocked on Pollock's door. Pollock was often too drunk or hung over to answer, but this time he did.

What happened next changed the history of art. "I was overwhelmed, bowled over, that's all," said Krasner. "I saw all those marvelous paintings. I felt as if the floor was sinking when I saw those paintings."

As Krasner described it, she fell in love with the art—and, almost incidentally, the artist. From that moment on, she devoted herself to nurturing and promoting Jackson Pollock—a task at which she succeeded spectacularly.

Before the decade was over, a *Life* magazine headline, spread across two pages with a picture of Pollock and his work, asked: "Is he the greatest living painter in the United States?" The question was in part a response to a statement by the critic Clement Greenberg, who called Pollock "the most powerful painter in contemporary America."

Greenberg left no doubt about Krasner's role, describing her as being the only one Pollock could talk to about his art and as having "the best eye in the country for the art of painting." He stated, "I don't feel Pollock would have gotten where he did without her eye and support."

Krasner was more than a professional partner, more than a wife, more than a lover. As Greenberg bluntly put it: "He couldn't do anything for himself. If he went to the train station to buy himself a ticket, he'd get drunk along the way."

Under these circumstances, there was obviously a cost to Pollock's success—and it was borne by Krasner. As she devoted herself fully to his life and art, her own work—once thought at least as promising as his—fell by the wayside. For years, she virtually stopped painting.

"In that household," said their friend, sculptor Reuben Kadish, "there was one painter and that was Jackson."

"Lee was kind of the opposite of competitive with Jackson," observed Elaine de Kooning, who, like Lee, was both a painter and a painter's wife. "She wiped herself out."

Was it worth it?

"That was what we thought we had to do in those days," said Patsy Southgate, a friend who was a writer and a writer's wife. "It was masochism, all right, but for turning out a Hemingway or a Pollock, it was well worth the candle."

Others were not so sure.

⁀—⁀

Jackson needed all the help he could get. His artistic training under the social realist Thomas Hart Benton already marked him as out of step with New York's increasingly abstract avant-garde. Before he met Lee, he had never made any money at his art. He lived with his brother, Sande, who supported him.

Lee's academic training far surpassed Jackson's, and she knew many more movers and shakers in the art world. She introduced him to artists, such as de Kooning and Arshile Gorky, and to critics, such as Greenberg and Harold Rosenberg. She acted as an intermediary between Jackson and gallery owner Peggy Guggenheim.

Jackson was uncomfortable talking about his art, especially when the discussions got too intellectual. Said the painter Paul Brach: "It's hard for him to take the floor with these guys. He's not articulate, he's very shy, he doesn't have it. But she does. She's his mouthpiece, and she can handle it beautifully."

Alone, the two did talk shop. "We really didn't do art talk . . . in the sense of talking about Matisse, his influence, etc.," Lee remembered. "This simply never existed in our life. He would . . . speak specifically of the painting in front of him."

Their friend John Bernard Meyers noted that the conversations between Lee and Jackson were in "the kind of shorthand people who are very close develop."

But it was in his personal life that Lee made the biggest difference. Soon after they met, she moved in with him. Sande gratefully ceded his role as roommate, and Lee became Jackson's financial and emotional bulwark.

She landed a job supervising artists who were painting camouflage for tanks and ships and designing World War II propaganda posters. She immediately hired Jackson—and made sure he didn't have much to do.

More importantly, Lee brought Jackson's drinking under control. She hosted lavish dinner parties, even though she'd never cooked before, so Jackson would stay home rather than go out to bars. She carefully invited friends who weren't likely to drink, and when they weren't available, she kept him busy herself. When these gambits didn't work, she'd sober him up in time to meet Guggenheim or others with influence in the art world.

Lee always thought of herself as a "city person." But in November 1945, to further remove Jackson from temptation, she convinced him to move to The Springs, a small village outside East Hampton. She secured a loan from Guggenheim, and they bought a farmhouse with a barn that they converted into a studio for Jackson. In deference to their new neighbors' conservative sensibilities, they also got married.

By the end of 1946, Jackson was more confident and secure—and more sober—than he'd ever been. He was also more productive; between then and 1950, he produced his greatest masterpieces.

It was in his studio-barn that Jackson developed the technique that assured his place in art history: the "drip" painting. First, he would lay the canvas flat on the floor. Then he would dip a long stick in a can of paint and wave it over the canvas. He would walk around the canvas, flinging paint from all sides.

In 1950, photographer Hans Namuth filmed Jackson at work, bringing him more acclaim. Namuth captured what he described as "the flame of explosion when the paint hits the canvas."

The drip paintings brought some ridicule as well. Readers answered *Life*'s question—Is Jackson Pollock the greatest living U.S. painter?—with questions of their own, ranging from "Is he a painter?" to "Why use the word 'living' so loosely?" The *Magazine of Art* compared his paintings to baked macaroni, and *Time* dubbed the artist "Jack the Dripper."

The meaning of the drip paintings has also sparked much debate. Some traced the technique to Navajo sand painters, others to jazz riffs. Cynics claimed he accidentally discovered the technique while he was drunk. In their Pulitzer Prize–winning biography, Steven Naifeh and Gregory White Smith argued that the artist was reenacting an early memory of his father urinating on a flat rock somewhere in the mountains of Arizona or California where Jackson grew up.

Another theory is that it was not his urine but his sperm that Jackson was figuratively flinging on the canvas. The critic William Feaver described the artist as "casting paint like seed," and *Time* reported that friends had seen him "emerge from the studio limp as a wet dish rag" and with "a cigarette smoldering on his lip."

The implication was that his relationship with Lee had given Jackson not just the security to paint, but the sexual confidence to bring his technique to fruition. As usual, Jackson himself said little—but what little he said certainly had some sexual connotations.

"The stuff is really beginning to flow," he said, soon after starting to make the drip paintings. "Grand feeling when it happens . . . I can literally be *in* the painting."

Regardless of their origins, regardless of their detractors, the drip paintings were undeniably an expression of the artist's emotions. And these were clearly powerful emotions, more powerfully expressed than in any abstract art anyone had seen.

No longer would Pollock or de Kooning or other abstract expressionists aspire to be included, as they did in 1941, in a show with French masters. The center of the avant-garde art world was now New York; indeed, it was now a tiny town outside East Hampton.

Lee's art, meanwhile, was nowhere to be seen, in either New York or the Hamptons. When they were in New York, taking care of Jackson occupied almost all her time. "My enthusiasm for his work," she once admitted, "was far greater than his for mine. . . . He did encourage me, but it was not the same kind of encouragement."

Lee began getting up early in the morning while Jackson was still asleep, so she could work. But she was suffering from acute artist's block. "The pigment would just build up into masses of gray sludge, and nothing happened," she recalled.

In The Springs, she started producing her *Little Image* series, paintings that shared many of the same characteristics as Jackson's larger works of the period. But no one was interested. It was Jackson's paintings that hung on the walls of the farmhouse; it was Jackson's paintings that dealers came to see. "I'd go visit them [and] there was Pollock, the main act," recalled Greenberg. "It was simply that she was the second one there."

One problem was the small size of Lee's paintings. Most of the great works of abstract expressionism were also large works. Jackson's were so big that he put his canvases on the floor, not an easel. But Jackson had the barn as his studio; Lee was limited to a small bedroom.

Why did Lee, who had once been so ambitious for herself, put up with this? Her own explanation, of course, was that she believed Jackson's greatness merited the sacrifice. "I couldn't run out and do a one-woman job on the whole masculine art world and continue my paintings and stay in the role I was in as Mrs. Pollock," she explained. The role of Mrs. Pollock was the role she chose.

Partly, too, the sexism of the art world was beyond her control. Critics, dealers, and other artists took women artists less seriously, and Lee certainly couldn't have changed that single-handedly.

But there were also psychological reasons for her putting Jackson first. In her own way, Lee was as insecure as he was. Her father had been remote and often nasty; so had her most serious boyfriend before Jackson, the Russian artist Igor Pantuhoff. Lee was not particularly attractive, adding to her doubts about herself.

So it was all the more remarkable that, during the early fifties, Lee started producing some of her best work. It was not all of a sudden: the *Little Image* paintings were already something of a breakthrough.

By June 1951, Jackson noticed a difference. "Lee is doing some of her best painting," he wrote a friend. "It has a freshness and bigness that she didn't get before."

For the first time, with obvious pride, Lee began signing her full name in a large script, instead of just putting "L.K." in tiny block letters.

She was also more aggressive in showing the work to visitors who'd come to see Jackson's. "She wasn't pushing Pollock as much anymore," recalled sculptor and painter Harry Jackson, who visited them in The Springs a number of times. "She was pushing Lee now."

Lee never rejected Jackson, as either wife or disciple. But it was clear that she was distancing herself from him. When she cut up some of his abandoned canvases to use in her collages, it was unclear whether it was an act of homage or hostility, albeit unconscious.

Jackson was certainly aware that Lee was no longer providing him the same kind of support, and it undoubtedly contributed to the artist's block that he now hit with a vengeance. He was too proud to repeat himself, but he had no idea how to follow up on the success of the drip paintings. He started painting entirely in black and trying less abstract approaches, the latter an apparent rejection of his own successes.

Only occasionally did these efforts approach the level of his earlier work, and Jackson knew it. Gradually, he stopped painting entirely.

A neighbor, the painter Conrad Marca-Relli, asked Jackson why he still bothered to go to the barn each day. Jackson answered: "I light the stove so the studio will be warm in case this is the day I can start to paint again."

Jackson also started drinking heavily. He was increasingly abusive toward Lee, though she later said the abuse was never physical. "He would just use more four-letter words than usual," she said. "Or he would take it out on the furniture."

But Lee was no longer willing to sacrifice everything to try to help Jackson. She began to think about divorce. Years later, she told of a dream she'd had during the difficult winter of 1955. "Jackson and I were standing on top of the world," she said. "The earth was a sphere with a pole going through the center, I was holding the pole with my right hand, and I was holding Jackson's hand with my left hand. Suddenly I let go of the pole, but I kept holding on to Jackson, and we both went floating off into outer space."

Lee never analyzed the dream, but its meaning seemed clear: the only way she could save herself was by letting go of Jackson's hand.

❦⸰—⸰❧

Jackson too was pulling away. In March 1956, he began an affair with a young artist named Ruth Kligman. In July, Lee discovered the two of them in Jackson's studio and decided it was time to leave her husband, at least temporarily. That same month, she boarded the *Queen Elizabeth* for a European vacation.

In August, Clement Greenberg called her in Paris to tell her that Jackson, probably drunk, had lost control of his car near their house in The Springs. He was dead, as was one of his passengers. The other passenger, Ruth Kligman, survived.

Lee felt grief-stricken and guilty, but she gradually learned to focus on the happier times with Jackson: "I remember sitting with Jackson on our country porch—sitting there for hours, looking into the landscape, and always at dusk, when the woods ahead turned into strange, mystifying shapes."

Lee lived another eighteen years, during which Jackson's work soared in value. She continued to devote a lot of time to his affairs, and when she died, her estate was worth $20 million.

But Lee devoted most of her time to her own painting, and her work after Jackson's death was bigger and better than anything she'd produced before. When she died, she was generally recognized as a leading abstract expressionist.

Most of the work that established her reputation was painted in the barn that had been Jackson's studio.

19

Johnny Cash and June Carter Cash

*J*ohnny Cash was an eighteen-year-old high school student in 1950 when he first saw June Carter, who was three years older, performing at the Grand Ole Opry. Recalled Johnny: "She was great. She was gorgeous. She was a star. I was smitten, seriously so."

June was not just a star, she was music royalty. She was a daughter of the Carter Family, a group whose songs, such as "Will the Circle Be Unbroken" and "Keep on the Sunny Side," inspired generations of country and folk singers.

By 1950, the original Carter Family—brothers A.P. and Ezra and their wives, Sara and Maybelle—had split up. June, the daughter of Ezra and Maybelle, was now part of an act known as Mother Maybelle and the Carter Sisters. She'd been performing with her sisters, Anita and Helen, since she was nine.

"I grew up on Mother Maybelle's singing," Johnny said. "I bet you that if you went around to the people who really *know* . . . you'd find a fair number of them willing to endorse Anita Carter as the greatest female country singer of them all."

But it was June who stuck in his head. "I'd liked what I heard of her on the radio," he said, "and I *really* liked what I saw of her from the balcony at the Ryman Auditorium."

Six years later, hits like "Folsom Prison Blues" and "I Walk The Line" had made Johnny a star in his own right, and he got up the nerve to approach June. This was backstage, again at the Opry.

"You and I are going to get married someday," he announced to her.

Understandably, June laughed.

"Well, good," she finally answered. "I can't wait."

◆•— —•◆

Another five years passed before Johnny made his next move. By now, he was the bigger star. He asked her to join his act, and soon they were touring together.

"I was enthralled," Johnny said. "Here was this vivacious, exuberant, funny, happy girl, as talented and spirited and strong-willed as they come, bringing out the best of me. . . . Life on the road improved immensely."

There were still a number of obstacles in the way of their romance, not the least of which was that both were married. Johnny's wife was the former Vivian Liberto. It was a troubled marriage, because Vivian hated the road and Johnny spent much of his time touring, but their three daughters held them together, at least loosely. June was married, also unhappily, to Rip Nix, and she had two daughters of her own.

Equally problematic, as June would quickly discover, was that the Man in Black—as Johnny was known—had a dark side. His famous line from "Folsom Prison Blues"—"I shot a man in Reno just to watch him die"—was of course purely fictional. In reality, Johnny had spent only a few days in jail, mostly after drug-related incidents.

But drugs were becoming a serious problem for him. He'd started taking amphetamines in 1957, then began drinking and taking barbiturates.

In addition to the jail stays, there were car crashes and hospitalizations. None of this led Johnny to let up on the drugs. "He demolished hotel rooms and stomped out the lights on the stage of the Grand Ole Opry," wrote Anthony DeCurtis, "while Keith Moon was still in short pants."

"Touring and drugs were what I did," Johnny recalled. "I was taking amphetamines by the handful, literally, and barbiturates by the handful too . . . just to stop the shaking from the amphetamines. I was canceling shows and recording dates, and when I did manage to show up, I couldn't sing because my throat was too dried out from the pills."

In spite of this, June found herself falling in love with Johnny. She expressed her feelings, a mix of lust and love and fear, in "Ring of Fire," a song that later became a huge hit for Johnny. "Love is a burning thing," it began. "And it makes a fiery ring/Bound by wild desire/I fell into a ring of fire."

June recalled, "One morning, about four o'clock, I was driving my car just about as fast as I could. I thought, 'Why am I out on the highway this time of night?' I was miserable, and it all came to me: 'I'm falling in love with somebody I have no right to fall in love with.

"I was frightened of his way of life," she continued. "I thought, 'I can't fall in love with this man, but it's just like a ring of fire.'"

Not wanting Johnny to know her feelings, June gave the song to her sister Anita to record. Johnny later claimed the ruse didn't fool him—he knew the song was about him. And he shared her feelings, both the love and the fear. "We hadn't said 'I love you.' We were both afraid to say it, because we knew what was going to happen: that eventually we were both going to be divorced, and we were going to go through hell. Which we did."

But the fire, Johnny added, did not turn out to be hell. "That was a kind of sweet fire," he said. "The ring of fire that I found myself in with June was the fire of redemption."

For when June finally decided she was in love with Johnny, she also decided she would get him off drugs.

⟪⟫—⟪⟫

Since they toured together, June could monitor Johnny's drug habit. Many of the drugs he was taking were legally prescribed, and she would make sure the doctors prescribing them knew Johnny was abusing them. She also found out where he hid his supply, and she'd flush the pills down the toilet.

At times, June despaired. "He is out of his head—his gourd is full—he is flying—his star is in the heavens—for a time," she said. "It is the codependent that is the sickest. . . . we are in the mire. . . .We are in the Ring of Fire and the flames are going higher."

Once, she gave up. Johnny remembered that they were in the Four Seasons Hotel in Toronto, sometime during the midsixties: "I don't know what exactly brought her to the point of leaving me. I'd been up for three or four days and I'd been giving her a really hard time, but that wasn't unusual. I guess there'd just been too much of it for her.

"We had adjoining rooms," he continued. "She came into mine and said, 'I'm going. I can't handle this anymore.'"

Johnny took her suitcase—and all her clothes—into his room. Then he locked the door, leaving June wearing nothing but a towel. "She promised not to leave if I gave her back her clothes, and I believed her, so I did," he said. "And through all the trials to come . . . she never tried to leave again."

June later wrote: "It took me a long time, and John as well, to crawl back up a cliff with no rope—a path with no stepping stones—a way with no will."

In early October 1967, Johnny was, as he described it, "scraping the filthy bottom of the barrel of life." He considered suicide.

"I knew what to do," he recalled. "I'd go into Nickajack Cave, on the Tennessee River just north of Chattanooga, and let God take me from this earth and put me wherever He puts people like me."

That was the turning point. Having remained a devout Christian even through his years of drug abuse, Johnny's mind turned to God. "He didn't speak to me—He never has, and I'll be very surprised if He ever does—but I do believe that at times he has put feelings in my heart and perhaps even ideas in my head," he later wrote. "There in Nickajack Cave I became conscious of a very clear, simple idea . . . I was going to die at God's time, not mine."

When he emerged from the cave, he told June and his mother that he was committed to getting off drugs. In November, Johnny performed at a benefit in Hendersonville, Tennessee. It was the first time in more than a decade that he'd performed straight.

"I'd been off pills for four weeks and felt like I'd be able to do it," he remembered. "I went onstage that evening with the worst case of butterflies I'd ever known."

Two months after the Hendersonville concert, he proposed—on stage in London, Ontario. Just as when years before he had announced his intentions to June backstage at the Opry, Johnny took her by surprise.

"Let's go on with the show," she said.

But this time, both were now divorced—and Johnny had an audience on his side. As fans called out "Say yes," June did so. The two broke into a Tim Hardin song.

"If I were a carpenter, and you were a lady/Would you marry me anyway, would you have my baby?" Johnny sang.

"If you were a carpenter, and I were a lady/I'd marry you anyway, I'd have your baby," June answered.

❦— —❧

The wedding took place in March 1968, just north of Nashville. That same year, Johnny released a live album, *At Folsom Prison*, and his biggest hit, "A Boy Named Sue."

The next year came "The Johnny Cash Show" on ABC. Johnny took the opportunity to extend Nashville's limits with guest appearances by, among others, Bob Dylan, Louis Armstrong, Linda Ronstadt, and the Who.

In 1970, June gave birth to John Carter Cash. "My happiness grew and grew," Johnny said.

But both his personal life and career would soon deteriorate. Though he never again took drugs in the same quantities as he had during the sixties, he began taking pills again in the seventies. He was in and out of clinics, including the Betty Ford Center.

"The hounds of hell are not going to stop snapping at your heels," he wrote. Again, Johnny turned to June, along with his children and his mother, all of whom confronted him in 1981. "I'm still absolutely convinced that the intervention was the hand of God working in my life," he later said.

"The publicity in the 1960s was that June saved my life, and I sometimes still hear it said that she's the reason I'm alive today," he continued. "That may be true, but knowing what I do about addiction and survival, I'm fully aware that the only human being who can save you is yourself. What June did for me was post signs along the way, lift me up when I was weak, encourage me when I was discouraged, and love me when I felt alone and unlovable."

The couple also faced the trauma of an armed robbery on Christmas Day 1982. Three men invaded their vacation home in Jamaica and held their eleven-year-old son at gunpoint for two hours while rummaging through the house. Police caught all three robbers, and the gunman was killed resisting arrest. But Johnny and June took years to recover.

"For quite a while I brooded," Johnny said. "I took sleeping pills, I carried a gun." The couple still has twenty-four-hour armed security guards at their Jamaican residence.

The seventies and eighties also saw Johnny struggle with his fading popularity. He had mixed emotions as his daughter Rosanne Cash emerged from his shadow and, for a while, surpassed him on the charts.

But in the nineties, Johnny staged a comeback, going, he recalled, from "has-been to hip icon." June also had a hit with new versions of Carter Family classics and her own songs, including "Ring of Fire."

And Johnny had yet another comeback in the late nineties, this time physically. In 1997, he was diagnosed with Shy-Drager syndrome, a rare and life-threatening neurological disorder something like Parkinson's disease. As with the struggle against drug addiction, both Johnny and June refused to give up.

Again, there were setbacks, and Johnny has been unable to go back on tour, but he has recovered to such an extent that some doctors have questioned whether the diagnosis was correct. "June told the doctors right away that I'd never accept a nasty-sounding disease like that," Johnny said in 2000. "She said I'd fight it and win, and she started praying right there. We both did."

"She has saved my life more than once," he said in another interview the same year. "She's always been there with her love, and it has certainly made me forget the pain for a long time, many times. When it gets dark, and everybody's gone home and the lights are turned off, it's just me and her."

20

John Lennon
and Yoko Ono

*F*or a while, she was the most despised woman in the world.

Little Richard, the rocker who appeared with John Lennon and Yoko Ono at a 1969 Toronto concert, remembered how the crowd reacted to her appearance: "People were throwing bottles at Yoko Ono. They were throwing everything at her. Finally she had to run off the stage. They would have beat her to death up there."

It was not her music they hated, though her highly experimental, minimalist compositions didn't win many fans. What Yoko had done was unforgivable: she was the woman who broke up the Beatles. "John was a hero to a lot of people and they just didn't want to give him up," Yoko later said.

The Beatles gave various explanations for the breakup over the years. But there was no question that Paul, George, and Ringo resented Yoko.

It was not, of course, that there had never been other women in John's life. Indeed, he had been married since 1962. But Cynthia Lennon knew her place. She didn't interfere when he slept with hundreds of other women on tour, and she certainly didn't interfere when the Beatles were recording.

One of the assistants in the studio later recalled, "John and Yoko were doing something the boys had never done before. I mean, the women simply did not appear."

Yoko didn't just appear; she actually had the nerve to give the Beatles advice about their performances. John was certain that Paul McCartney was sending a clear message when, during the recording of the *White Album*, he sang the chorus, "Get back! Get back! Get back to where you once belonged!"

Recalled John: "Every time he sang the line in the studio, he'd look at Yoko."

&*— —*&

Yoko, before she met John, was sort of a semicelebrity, known mostly in the world of avant-garde art. The daughter of a wealthy banker, she had grown up first in Japan and then in Scarsdale, but she was living a bohemian life in New York. She had performed with such famous composers as John Cage, as well as in the dance company of Merce Cunningham, but she was best known for what later came to be called "concept art."

In 1961, her one-woman show at a Madison Avenue gallery featured her "instruction paintings." In one, for example, visitors were instructed to walk on an empty canvas on the floor. This was called *Painting to be Stepped On*. Another, *Kitchen Piece*, instructed viewers to throw leftover food at a blank canvas on the wall.

Yoko later achieved more notoriety for a film she produced with her then-husband, Tony Cox. This was *Bottoms*, which featured the buttocks of 365 unidentified men and women. The mainstream press could not resist reporting on the "bottomless indignation" of the viewing public.

So it should have come as no surprise that John Lennon, who had been a serious art student before giving it up for the Beatles and who was the most avant-garde of the foursome, showed up at London's Indica Gallery on November 9, 1966, for a preview of Yoko's latest exhibit, Unfinished Paintings and Objects.

Following the artist's written instructions, John climbed a ladder toward a canvas attached to the ceiling. Then he looked through a magnifying glass and read, printed on the canvas in tiny letters, "Yes."

"That was the first piece of mine that he saw," Yoko recalled. "He told me later that he loved it because it was so positive and that at last there was someone who thought like he did. If it had said 'No,' then he probably wouldn't have looked at the rest of the show."

Next, John turned to a jar of nails and a hammer, where the instructions were to "hammer a nail in." John asked Yoko if he could do so. She told him to go ahead, but it would cost him two shillings.

Smiling, John answered, "I'll give you an imaginary two shillings and hammer an imaginary nail."

Then he spotted an apple on a pedestal and noted the £200 price tag. He took a bite and put the apple back.

Yoko later claimed she had no idea that she was talking to the famous Beatle. Some of their more cynical biographers were convinced otherwise: they have claimed that she knew perfectly well who he was and that their first encounter was a carefully planned and perfectly executed effort to ensnare a wealthy patron.

Either way, there's no question they intrigued each other. John was impressed by Yoko's radical, yet playful, approach to her work. After years of groupies, here was a woman who truly understood art.

"I just realized she knew everything I knew, and probably more," John recalled. "And it was coming out of a *woman's* head. It just sort of bowled me over."

"It was like man meets Woman on common ground and East meets West and all the rest," Yoko agreed.

John and Yoko began seeing each other in what was, at first, a purely intellectual relationship. He sponsored her art exhibits and held one of his own, You Are Here, which clearly showed her influence.

"As she was talking to me, I would get high, and the discussion would get to such a level that I would be going higher and higher," John said. "When she'd leave, I'd go back to this sort of suburbia. Then I'd meet her again and my head would go open like I was on an acid trip."

It was while they were on an actual acid trip—in May 1968— that John and Yoko spent a night together.

"I didn't realize I was in love with her. I was still thinking it was an artistic collaboration," he recalled. "Yoko came to visit me and we took some acid. I was always shy with her, and she was shy, so . . . we went upstairs and made tapes. . . . And then as the sun rose we made love."

Cynthia Lennon, who'd been away on vacation, arrived home to find John in his robe and Yoko in Cynthia's kimono. Both marriages were now over—Cynthia divorced John in November, and Tony Cox divorced Yoko the following February.

In November, John and Yoko released the result of their all-night recording session: *Unfinished Music No. 1: Two Virgins*. Neither the critics nor the public knew what to make of the strange improvisational sounds, but the music didn't really matter. Most of the attention focused on the album's cover, which was a photo of John and Yoko, both completely naked.

As if the photo weren't provocative enough, on the day John and Yoko had planned a press conference on the album, police charged both with possession of marijuana.

John once sang, and no doubt believed, that "all you need is love." But by the end of 1968, the love of John and Yoko had alienated both their spouses, all of the Beatles, and the majority of his fans.

❧·— ·❧

It was unfair to put all the blame for the Beatles' breakup on Yoko. Even before John met her, the group had stopped touring together and started drifting apart. The songs were no longer the joint productions they'd once been. As early as 1966, all four were composing on their own, then arriving in the studio with the songs almost done.

George Harrison and Ringo Starr were both bored with the Beatles, and Harrison in particular was increasingly drawn to Indian music and culture.

Business differences were tearing apart the group too. Paul McCartney wanted his future father-in-law, Lee Eastman, to handle the finances. John and the others turned instead to the Rolling Stones' manager, Allen Klein.

Moreover, though Yoko was undeniably difficult to deal with, there was also an element of sexism in the Beatles' refusal to take anything she had to say seriously. "The Beatles were used to situations where they were closer to each other than to their women," Yoko later said. "I was not aware of that. But I don't think you could have broken up four very strong people like them, even if you tried. So there must have been something that happened within them—not an outside force at all."

Still, there was no denying Yoko's role in the band's demise. As John explained it: "When I met Yoko is when you meet your first woman and you leave the guys and the bar and you don't go play football anymore. . . . Maybe some guys like to do it every Friday night or something and continue that relationship with the boys, but once I found *the* woman, the boys became of no interest whatsoever, other than they were like old friends.

"It so happened," he continued, "that these boys were well known and weren't just the local guys at the bar. These were guys everybody else knew. But it was the same thing."

In any case, there was no going back. John was soon divorced from the Beatles as well as Cynthia. There was no reason not to remarry, and on March 12, 1969, John and Yoko did so. The ceremony was held on the Rock of Gibraltar, which had the unique advantage of being part of the British Commonwealth but not having a press corps.

If anyone thought that meant John and Yoko would now seek a quiet respectability, the honeymoon quickly proved otherwise.

❦— —❧

Two weeks after their wedding, John and Yoko staged their first "bed-in." For seven days, the couple opened up their room at the Amsterdam Hilton to reporters.

Many of these reporters, who after the *Two Virgins* album cover figured the next step was for the couple to have sex in public, were disappointed. John and Yoko were indeed in bed, but they were there to talk about peace, not love. John introduced the press to "Give Peace a Chance," the tune that became the anthem of the antiwar movement.

The bed-ins, first in Amsterdam and then a couple of months later in Toronto, did nothing to change John and Yoko's image as flakes. Even the antiwar press questioned whether bed-ins were an effective contribution to the movement. But they were, if nothing else, a clear signal that John and Yoko together were as committed to the avant-garde as Yoko alone had been.

They followed up the bed-ins with a series of films, including *Smile* (in which John smiles) and *Two Virgins* (in which John's face is transformed into Yoko's). Then came an exhibit at a Syracuse Museum, This Is Not Here, which featured an "eternal clock" (with no hands), an all-white chess set, and blank canvases for visitors to paint on.

Some of these productions were radical in an artistic sense alone. But enough of them were sufficiently political to draw the ire of the Nixon administration. Citing John's 1968 drug conviction, the Immigration and Naturalization Service began deportation proceedings in March 1972.

The deportation attempt ultimately failed when the New York Supreme Court determined that it was politically motivated. But it took its toll on John and Yoko. In October 1973, the couple separated. John moved to Los Angeles, and Yoko stayed in New York.

The deportation proceedings were by no means the only stresses breaking them apart. Years of bad press, doubts about their artistic directions, and frequent drinking and drug use also played a role.

For Yoko, who was extremely proud of her work, it was humiliating to still be thought of primarily as John's wife. "I thought I wanted to be free from being Mrs. Lennon," she recalled. "Before that I was doing all right, thank you. My work might not have been selling much, I might have been poorer, whatever. But I had my human pride intact and I was doing all right.

"I was used to being an artist and free and all that, and when I got together with John, because we're always in the public eye, I lost the freedom," she added. "I needed the space to think."

As for John, though he never publicly criticized Yoko, it must have become a strain to live with her powerful ego—this was, after all, the woman who felt she could tell the Beatles how to improve their music. John continued to admire her work, but he must have sometimes longed for the days when he lived with and slept with many far less demanding women.

He apparently recaptured some of that in California, where he lived with the couple's former secretary, May Pang. She was ten years younger than John and idolized him.

The separation, which John later referred to as the "lost weekend," lasted eighteen months. But the two stayed in regular phone contact throughout, often speaking many times a day, and they never began divorce proceedings. In November 1974, after Yoko saw John perform with Elton John at Madison Square Garden, the two spoke backstage. Two months later, John returned home.

Announced John: "Yoko and I are proud to say that our separation was a failure."

❖—❖

Just a few days after John's return, Yoko, then forty-two, was pregnant. The birth of their son Sean in October 1975 ushered in a new phase in the couple's relationship, one in which John played the role of a feminist father—or, as he called it, a "house-husband"—while Yoko handled the family finances.

"I've been breaking bread," John explained, when asked by a reporter what he'd been doing, "and looking after the baby."

"With what secret projects going on in the basement?" persisted the interviewer, David Sheff.

"Are you kidding?" John responded. "Bread and babies, as every housewife knows, is a full-time job. . . . It is such a tremendous responsibility to see that the baby has the right amount of food and doesn't overeat and gets the right amount of sleep."

Pushed further, John conceded that, unlike most housewives, he had the help of a cook and a nanny. "I'm a rich housewife," he said. "But it still involves caring, and making sure the sheets are being looked after by whomever I employ, and the staff all come to me with their problems. They don't go bothering Yoko, because she's dealing with the money."

In 1980, John took a break from raising Sean to work on *Double Fantasy*, which turned out to be his final album. On December 8, as he and Yoko left their apartment, John was shot and killed by a deranged fan for whom he'd signed a copy of the album earlier that day.

It's impossible to tell, therefore, what direction he and Yoko might have taken next. Very little in their past had been predictable, and the new album seemed an indication that they would have continued to surprise and entertain both their fans and their detractors.

In an interview published just after his death, John made clear that he was looking forward to whatever the future held. "I *don't* believe in yesterday, by the way," he said.

BARNSTORMERS, BANK
ROBBERS, AND BALLPLAYERS

21

Anne Morrow Lindbergh and Charles Lindbergh

*F*light, for aviation's most famous couple, was as much a way of life as a way to get someplace. For Charles Lindbergh, the first pilot to cross the Atlantic solo, that blend of technology and daring turned him into America's hero, a celebrity unlike any before or since. For Anne Morrow Lindbergh, flying was an apt metaphor for her life; never quite sure whether she was her husband's copilot or flight attendant, she struggled to be both a wife and a writer, and ended up writing one of the bestselling and most-beloved books about marriage.

Together, the Lindberghs soared higher than any famous couple in history. And when that celebrity turned against them, theirs was a crash landing unlike any other. First there was the kidnapping and murder of their child. Then there was Charles's role as the leading spokesman for isolationism, which ultimately left him as reviled as he'd once been revered.

No wonder flight also came to be, for the Lindberghs, a means of escape—from the press, the public, the world below. The question was whether they would flee separately or together, whether even a love as strong as theirs could survive so many ups and downs.

❦·—·❧

Charles Lindbergh was not the first to fly across the Atlantic; in 1919, two British pilots made it from Newfoundland to Ireland. But Lindbergh was the first to make it to the continent, and his

1927 trip from New York to Paris was a good fifteen hundred miles farther than anyone had flown before. What's more, he made the 33½-hour trip alone.

More than 150,000 Parisians swarmed around the single-engine *Spirit of St. Louis* as Lindbergh landed, and more acclaim followed. The story of his trip became a bestseller, *We*; he was offered millions to star in a movie about his life. "People behaved," his biographer A. Scott Berg remarked, "as though Lindbergh had walked on water, not flown over it."

He was, without doubt, the world's most eligible bachelor. So when he decided it was time to get married, he didn't anticipate any problems.

"Somewhere down on the surface of the earth was the girl I would marry," he recalled in his autobiography. "It was simply a case of swooping down at the right place to find her."

Practical as always, Charles listed the qualities he was looking for in a woman: good health, good form, good sight and hearing. It was no different, he thought, than writing up the specifications for an airplane.

In reality, it wasn't so easy. Sure, there were plenty of women eager to meet him. But with the press following his every move, any date would make an instant headline. Moreover, Charles was extraordinarily shy and inexperienced with women; by his own later admission, he'd never asked one out.

"Girls were everywhere," he conceded, "but it was hard to get to know them."

Then an opportunity presented itself. Dwight Morrow, a J. P. Morgan partner who acted as Charles's financial advisor and was U. S. ambassador to Mexico, asked him to fly to Mexico City as a gesture to ease tensions between the two countries. Charles agreed.

In December, Lindbergh headed south, but the great navigator got a bit lost. To check what town he was over, he swooped down over the nearest railroad station and read a sign posted on the adobe wall. It read "Caballeros." Yet there was no Caballeros on his map. Eventually, Charles realized that it was a sign for the men's room, and eventually he landed in Mexico City.

After making his way through the usual crowds, he stayed at the ambassador's home. A week later, the Morrows' middle daughter, Anne, arrived home from Smith College for her Christmas break.

It was not love at first sight.

"We were a little annoyed," Anne wrote in her December 21, 1927, diary entry. "All this public-hero stuff breaking into our family party. A regular newspaper hero, the baseball player-type—a nice man, perhaps, but not of my world at all."

Indeed not. Anne's world—that of a child of a partner of J. P. Morgan—was as secluded as Charles's was now public. Moreover, Anne already aspired to be a writer, and Charles was, as she put it, "not at all intellectual." It was Anne's older sister, Elisabeth, who was far more outgoing and strikingly beautiful, whom everyone thought might catch Charles's attention. Not shy, bookish Anne.

"You want to write!" Charles said after Anne told him of her ambition. "I want to do the things other people write about!"

Yet their different worlds seemed to merge when seen from above. Charles invited the Morrows for a flight, and soon Anne was in love.

On Christmas Day, she wrote in her diary: "The idea of this clear, direct, straight boy—how it has swept out of sight all other men I have ever known, all the pseudo-intellectuals, the sophisticates, the posers. My world—my little embroidery-beribboned world is smashed."

Anne had made an impression on Charles as well. But it took until the following October for him to summon up the courage to ask her for a date—the first date he'd ever made. As always, he thought things through in advance. He knew she'd enjoyed their flight in Mexico, so he invited her flying again.

They couldn't say much, because the sound of the engine drowned out any conversation. But they were both thrilled to be in the air, and Anne discovered that under Charles's tutelage she—who had just learned to drive a car—could fly a plane.

"I can't explain to you, Con, what a change had come in my attitude—just from that hour ride out," she wrote to her other sister on October 16, 1928. "I discovered that I wasn't a bit afraid of him or even worshipful any more. That Norse god has just gone. He's just terribly kind and absolutely natural."

Charles was more matter-of-fact in his autobiography. "Our ground date a few days later involved an afternoon and evening drive over roads of New Jersey," he wrote. "When it was over we were engaged to be married."

←— —→

To keep away reporters, the wedding plans were kept top secret. A Morrow family seamstress prepared Anne's dress, Elisabeth picked the flowers for her sister's bouquet from the grounds of the family's estate, and the wedding cake was smuggled into the house. None of Charles's friends were present; there was no best man. Charles and Anne left in a borrowed car, with Anne hiding in the backseat.

Only after they were gone did Dwight Morrow's secretary read aloud to the reporters at the gate: "Mr. and Mrs. Dwight W. Morrow announce the marriage of their daughter Anne to Charles A. Lindbergh at Englewood, New Jersey, May 27, 1929."

Anticipating that reporters would expect them to honeymoon by airplane, Charles and Anne snuck aboard a thirty-eight-foot motorboat and headed up the Atlantic coast. They didn't have long to savor their privacy. Two days later, they were spotted at Block Island, and the rest of their honeymoon was spent fleeing reporters and photographers who pursued them in boats and planes.

So Charles and Anne took to the air and ended up spending many of the early years of their marriage there. "We had no home; we lived in hotels, planes, or other people's homes," Anne later recalled. "We traveled constantly back and forth across the

United States laying out the new Transcontinental Air Transport passenger route between New York and Los Angeles, or inaugurating new Pan American Airways routes to Central and South America."

For Anne, who had grown up in a family for whom travel meant lots of luggage carried by lots of servants, Charles's pioneering was something of a shock. But she loved it. She established a long-distance record for radio communication between an airplane and a ground station, she became a competent pilot, and she was the first woman to earn a glider's license.

"I adored the flying," she later wrote. "It was freedom and beauty and escape from crowds."

Anne continued to copilot for Charles, even after she became pregnant. Just two months before the birth of Charles Jr., the couple flew east across the country, breaking the transcontinental speed record.

❧— —❧

The birth of their son gave Anne and Charles a reason to settle down a bit in their new home outside Hopewell, New Jersey. Charles Jr. was a beautiful, happy baby who loved playing with his parents, especially when his father swung him through the air. Anne would soon become pregnant with their second child, another boy.

Then came one of the most traumatic events any parent could endure. On March 1, 1932, Charles Jr. was kidnapped from the

Hopewell nursery. The kidnappers left behind a ransom note demanding $50,000.

Colonel Norman Schwarzkopf of the New Jersey State Police (and the father of the future Desert Storm commander) took command of the investigation. All sorts of con men and gangsters came out of the woodwork, offering to help; even Al Capone, from his prison cell, promised he could find the baby—in return for his freedom. In April, Charles paid the ransom to a man who in turn gave them a note telling them where to find the baby, but a search of the area turned up nothing.

Seven weeks later, the baby's body was found just a few miles from the Hopewell house.

Charles and Anne expressed their grief differently. Ever a man of action, Charles threw himself into the investigation, working closely with Schwarzkopf. Anne expressed her agony in her diaries, writing: "I'll never believe in anything again . . . faith and goodness and security in life."

Anne had nowhere to turn. When she tried to talk to Charles, he responded curtly, "I can't go through it again."

"There is the difference between men and women," she wrote in the February 15, 1933, entry in her diary. "I never went through it really then. I never accepted it. I never experienced it and I will never be through with it."

The 1935 arrest and trial of Bruno Richard Hauptmann only made matters worse. Charles continued to focus all his energies on the case, turning his sorrow into anger that was sometimes directed at Anne. Anne's mother wrote in her diary: "Anne came into my room with tears in her eyes. He loves her, but he wants to reform her—make her over into his own practical scientific mold."

Hauptmann's conviction brought no relief. Reporters continued to stake out the Lindberghs' home, to follow them wherever they went. In the fall of 1935, photographers chased a car carrying the Lindbergh's second son, Jon, now three, on his way home from school. They forced the car to the side of the road, then jumped out and stuck cameras in the terrified child's face.

For the Lindberghs, it was the final straw. Charles and Anne decided to move to England.

The move brought some relief from the press, but it also took Charles down the path that would destroy his reputation in America. Disillusioned by the kidnapping, the press harassment, and the carnival atmosphere that surrounded Hauptmann's trial, Charles was seduced by the sense of order he saw in Nazi Germany. He stopped short of moving to Germany or embracing Nazism, but his warnings about German power and his leadership of America First—an organization devoted to keeping the United States out of World War II—branded him a traitor in the eyes of many Americans.

"In just fifteen years," Anne's sister Constance later commented, "he had gone from Jesus to Judas."

Anne's loyalties were torn. Privately, she questioned her husband's positions, but she couldn't bring herself to distance herself from him publicly. Indeed, she threw her writing energy behind him, penning a defense of isolationism that described fascism as the "wave of the future" and warned America to get out of its way. It was by no means an endorsement of fascism, but Anne too was labeled a Nazi sympathizer.

After the United States entered the war, Charles partially redeemed his reputation by contributing to the war effort. He developed techniques that increased the altitude and range of American planes and then flew fifty combat missions in the South Pacific. The latter required various military officers to look the other way, since President Roosevelt, still furious at Lindbergh's earlier isolationism, refused to let him officially enlist.

In 1953, Charles completed his comeback with the publication of *The Spirit of St. Louis*, an account of his transatlantic voyage. Unlike his quickie 1927 book, this one was taut and stirring. It became a huge bestseller and a movie starring Jimmy Stewart. In 1954, the book won the Pulitzer Prize.

Anne wanted to share in Charles's happiness, but she couldn't. After all, *she* was supposed to be the writer in the family. Yet all she had to show for it was the isolationist credo *The Wave of the Future*, a book that ranked in many minds next to *Mein Kampf*. She had helped Charles write his book and had gotten nothing but a dedication out of it.

She was tired of standing in Charles's shadow. She was tired of his flying off anytime he pleased and leaving her to take care of their five kids. She was tired of his need to control everything around him, everything she did, even what she bought. (After all, she had a healthy trust fund and didn't need his money.) She was tired of being his copilot.

"The Great Man—the Great Epic—the Great Author etc. etc.," Anne muttered in her diary. "I am living in the aura of 1929. Only I am different."

❦— —❧

How could she choose between being a wife and a writer? Anne struggled with the question and then found a way to be both.

She began to write about a shell—a delicate bivalve called the "double sunrise."

"How beautiful it is," she wrote. "Two people listening to each other, two shells meeting each other, making one world between them. There are no others in the perfect unity of that instant, no other people or things or interests."

Such had once been her love for Charles. But then, "how inevitably the perfect unity is invaded; the relationship changes; it becomes complicated, encumbered by its contact with the world."

And so Anne sought, again in shells, other models for a marriage. There was, for example, the oyster: "Sprawling and uneven, it has the irregularity of something growing. It looks rather like the house of a big family, pushing out one addition after another to hold its teeming life—here a sleeping porch for the children, and there a veranda for the play-pen; here a garage for the extra car and there a shed for the bicycles."

Or there was that rare creature, the "argonauta," which is not fastened to its shell at all. "Can we middle-aged argonauts when we outgrow the oyster bed, look forward to the freedom of the nautilus who has left its shell for the open seas?" Anne asked. "I believe there is, after the oyster bed, an opportunity for the best relationship of all: not a limited, mutually exclusive one, like the sunrise shell; and not a functional, dependent one, as in the oyster bed; but the meeting of two whole fully developed people as persons."

Anne's 1955 book, *Gift from the Sea*, was not quite a feminist manifesto, since it argued that women could best find freedom through marriage. But it was most definitely a different kind of marriage than she or most women had in the fifties. The book was a declaration both of independence and of loyalty.

Gift from the Sea struck a chord in prefeminist America. Its sales far surpassed those of Charles's book, making it number one on the bestseller list for a year. It was as beloved as *Wave of the Future* had been despised. Anne was no longer Charles's copilot; she was a famous author in her own right.

And Charles and Anne, as much as any couple, lived the marriage about which she wrote in *Gift from the Sea*. He continued to fly; she continued to write; and though they often found themselves on opposite sides of the globe, their time together remained not just loving, but essential to their independent lives.

The Lindberghs' daughter Reeve, in her own eloquent memoir, said it best: "It was not a simple romance, and it was sometimes an uneasy and uncomfortable union, but my belief, nonetheless, is that neither one of my parents felt fully alive, or truly like himself or herself, unless the other one was there."

22

Amelia Earhart and G. P. Putnam

*H*istory has cast plenty of women in supporting roles. "She was his muse," say the biographers, if the man was an artist. Or "she was the power behind the throne," they say, if he was a king. Much rarer is it a man whose glory is reflected.

At first glance, G. P. Putnam seemed an unlikely candidate for such a role. For one thing, he loved to be in the limelight. At the firm that bore his grandfather's name, G.P. specialized in publishing bestsellers written by celebrities—among them Charles Lindbergh, the first man to make a solo flight across the Atlantic, and Richard Byrd, who led an expedition to the North Pole. Putnam and his wife Dorothy hosted lavish parties for his authors at their Rye, New York, mansion.

Moreover, G.P. was every bit as much an adventurer as any of his authors. He organized and joined expeditions to Greenland and Baffin Island. He was as brilliant a publicist as he was a publisher, but definitely not the type to stay quietly behind the scenes.

Besides, Amelia Earhart seemed to have little need for anyone to prop her up. Her achievements spoke for themselves: first woman to lead a flight across the Atlantic in 1928; first woman to make a round-trip solo flight across the United States, also in 1928; first woman to fly solo across the Atlantic in 1932; and first person to fly solo from Hawaii to California in 1935.

And yet, history has cast Putnam as Earhart's Svengali. "If G.P. needed to bask in her limelight, she needed him to maintain that limelight," wrote Doris Rich, one of her biographers. "He would take care of the 'grubby' work."

Amelia piloted the planes, but it was G.P. who navigated her career. He arranged the financing for her flights, publicized her name, and pushed her to go for record after record.

Rich called it "a marriage of convenience." Gore Vidal, whose father Gene was a close friend of both Amelia and G.P., said simply, "she married her manager."

"She was a Putnam-manufactured commodity before she did any of those things," concluded the New York *Daily News*, "and arguably she might never have been in a position to do them at all had Putnam not so invented her in the first place."

The most damning criticism of the Earhart-Putnam marriage—or partnership, as its more cynical observers preferred to call it—had to do with Amelia's last flight, an attempt to travel around the world via the equator. The trip ended in July 1937 when Amelia disappeared somewhere over the Pacific.

Amelia's fate remains one of history's most intriguing mysteries, inspiring all sorts of speculation. One theory blames G.P. for her disappearance: he had organized a big welcome for Amelia in Los Angeles on July 4; even though neither she nor the plane was ready, he supposedly pressured her to take off and stay on schedule.

This story is unfair both to Putnam and to Earhart, as are most of the portraits that reduce him to a huckster and her to his product. They ignore the fact that G.P. and Amelia were not just partners, but lovers. Theirs was, to be sure, a love that strayed far from the usual idea of romance. It was a love that was complicated by Amelia's dedication to flying and feminism, as well as by their business partnership.

But it was most definitely a love that both of them felt deeply.

←·—·→

There's no denying that when G.P. first saw Amelia, he thought of her as a promising business opportunity.

After turning Lindbergh's story of his 1927 flight into a best-seller, G.P. was in the market for another adventure story. He heard that a woman named Amy Guest was planning to sponsor a woman's flight across the Atlantic. Guest had originally wanted to make the trip herself, but her family talked her out of it. So G.P. offered to help find the "right sort of girl."

He soon heard about Amelia, then a Boston social worker who flew for sport. He invited her to New York for an interview. Impressed, he took her over to meet David Layman, who represented Guest.

"Why do you want to fly the Atlantic?" Layman asked, coming right to the point.

"Why," she replied, "does a man ride a horse?"

"Because he wants to, I guess."

"Well, then."

Amelia got the job. On June 17, she took off from Newfoundland, and twenty hours and forty minutes later she landed in Wales. Amelia had actually been little more than a passenger; she was neither pilot nor navigator. But she was hailed as "Lady Lindbergh" and became an instant celebrity.

G.P. went right to work. He struck deals with the *New York Times* and Paramount for the newspaper and newsreel versions of her story. He arranged lecture tours. Soon she was endorsing everything from Kodak film to Pratt & Whitney engines and her own line of clothing and luggage.

By July, Amelia was living with G.P. and his wife Dorothy in their Rye home so he could help her churn out a book, to be called *20 Hrs., 40 Min*. The book was soon published by, of course, Putnam's.

At first, then, their relationship was strictly business. G.P.'s wife Dorothy, after all, was also living in the house; indeed, she and Amelia became friends. And Amelia was, at least officially, engaged at the time, though her fiancé remained in Massachusetts and rarely saw her.

Gradually, however, the business relationship turned into friendship and then love.

"We both loved the outdoors, books and sport," Amelia recalled. "And so we lunched together, and dined together, took long horseback rides together. We came to depend on each other, yet it was only friendship between us, or so—at least— I thought at first.

"At last the time came, I don't know quite when it happened," she continued, "when I could deceive myself no longer. I couldn't continue telling myself that what I felt for G.P. was only friendship."

In November 1928, Amelia called off her engagement. In December 1929, Dorothy divorced G.P. Amelia was undoubtedly one reason for the end of the Putnams' marriage, but by no means the only one: Dorothy was also in love, and she remarried soon after.

G.P. and Amelia were now free to marry. But Amelia hesitated. She feared marriage might spell the end of her flying career.

"I am still unsold on marriage," she wrote a friend. "I don't want *anything*, all the time."

Amelia compared marriage to living in a den: "A den is stuffy. I'd rather live in a tree. . . . I think I may not ever be able to see marriage except as a cage until I am unfit to work or fly or be active—and of course I wouldn't be desirable then."

G.P., as persistent and persuasive as any man, proposed at least twice, by some accounts six times. Eventually, he wore Amelia down. On February 7, 1931, the couple was married at the home of G.P.'s mother.

Lest there be any doubt about her continued independence, however, immediately after the ceremony, Amelia slipped off her wedding ring. She never wore it again.

◆•—•◆

Just before the ceremony, Amelia handed G.P. a note she'd hastily written on her future mother-in-law's stationery. It is a startlingly frank expression of her ambivalence about marriage:

Dear G.P.;

There are some things which should be writ before we are married. Things we have talked over before—most of them. You must know again my reluctance to marry, my feeling that I shatter thereby chances in work which means so much to me. I feel the move just now as foolish as anything I could do. I know there may be compensations, but have no heart to look ahead. In our life together I shall not hold you to any medieval code of faithfulness to me, nor shall I consider myself bound to you similarly. If we can be honest I think the difficulties which arise may be best avoided. . . .

Please let us not interfere with the other's work or play, nor let the world see our private joys or disagreements. In this connection I may have to keep some place where I can go to be myself now and then, for I cannot guarantee to endure at all the confinements of even an attractive cage.

I must exact a cruel promise, and that is you will let me go in a year if we find no happiness together. . . .

Most commentators have focused on Amelia's demand for a sexually open marriage, and it is indeed startling. But, though some of her biographers have argued Amelia later had a brief affair with Gene Vidal, there's no hard evidence she was ever unfaithful. Gore Vidal, for one, thought the relationship with his father was platonic.

Less sensational, but equally striking in its own way, was Amelia's more general declaration of independence. Even as the most famous woman flier in the world, even marrying the man who had helped make her reputation, Amelia was clearly terrified that marriage would tether her to earth—and to G.P.

G.P., who didn't reveal the existence of the letter until after Amelia's death, described it as "a sad little letter, brutal in its frankness, but beautiful in its honesty."

The letter is also, for all its ambivalence, compelling evidence that Amelia loved G.P. and that this was not a "marriage of convenience." Clearly, Amelia on her wedding day was not thinking about how G.P. could help her career. On the contrary, she saw marriage—understandably, in those prefeminist times—as an impediment to her career. That she overcame her fears and went ahead with it is perhaps the best evidence of the depth of her feelings for him.

As for G.P., he also deserves credit for overcoming whatever reservations he must have felt on being presented with such an unusual prenuptial agreement. He too was deeply in love.

◆•— —•◆

The cage Amelia feared never materialized. Just two weeks after getting married, Amelia wrote her mother: "I am much happier than I expected I could ever be in that state. I believe the whole thing was for the best . . . I haven't changed at all and will only be busier I suppose . . ."

Amelia and G.P. enjoyed each other's company. "I would rather play and work with you than with anyone I have yet encountered or could imagine—comb that out of your carefully tousled hair," he wrote her.

She wrote him a poem that began: "To touch your hand or see your face today/Is joy."

That Amelia's independence was not lost amid taking care of housework or kids was, admittedly, in part because the couple had servants for the former and none of the latter. But it was also because they worked well together.

G.P. continued to raise funds for her flights and to arrange lectures and endorsements, but she remained in control of her own career. "He trusts my judgment about my ship, just as I trust his about books," she said in a 1932 interview.

"In the routine meaning of the term I was, I suppose, A.E.'s manager," G.P wrote. But he added, "Philosophically, as has been said, she felt no human being of normal intelligence should be *managed* by anyone else. Temperamentally she had a healthy distaste for the implication of being led around by the hand. Yet no client of any counselor ever received counsel more reasonably—or, on occasion, refused with more firmness to act on it!"

In 1932, when Amelia decided to fly the Atlantic solo—thus answering those critics who'd emphasized she'd been just a passenger on the previous crossing—G.P. raised the money and cleverly scheduled her departure for the day five years after Lindbergh's.

And in 1937, when Amelia decided to fly around the world, G.P. again made the arrangements. But he certainly didn't pressure her to leave unprepared; on the contrary, he made clear she could back out at any time.

Just before she left, he wrote her: "You know I sympathize fully with your ambition and will abet it, and 98% I know you'll get away with it. But we both recognize the hazards, and I love you dearly—I don't want to run the risk of perhaps having to go on without you. . ."

If her husband didn't pressure her into it, why did Amelia risk her final, fatal flight? Some have speculated she was a spy, and that the trip was merely a cover for her to photograph Japanese installations in the Pacific. But that seems unlikely, especially since Amelia was a pacifist.

In the journal she kept (which she cabled to G.P. from various stops along the way so it would be ready for publication right after the trip was over), she clearly explained her reasons for the trip: "Here was shining adventure, beckoning with new experiences . . . Then too there was my belief that now and then women should do for themselves what men have already done—and occasionally what men have not done . . . perhaps encouraging other women toward greater independence of thought and action."

What propelled Amelia then, as always, was her commitment to feminism and, above all, her love of flying. From Karachi, more than halfway around the world, Amelia phoned G.P., who asked her if she was having a good time.

"You betcha!" she answered. "It's a grand trip. We'll do it again, together, sometime."

❧

When Amelia and her plane vanished, President Franklin Roosevelt ordered a massive naval search. It lasted one week, cost $4 million, and covered approximately 250,000 miles—to no avail.

Officials concluded Amelia had run out of gas and gone down somewhere in the ocean. But G.P was not satisfied. He financed additional searches, tracking down a series of false leads and becoming the victim of several hoaxes. Two years after her disappearance, he finally declared Amelia legally dead.

The search for his wife cost G.P. much of his personal fortune. In the end, he had to sell his home in Rye to pay his bills. Years later, G.P.'s granddaughter, Sally Putnam Chapman, found among his papers a 1938 letter of resignation from the Explorers Club in New York. This too may have been a cost-saving measure.

Or it may have been that he simply lost the heart for any more explorations.

23

Clyde Barrow and Bonnie Parker

*T*hey stuck up mostly gas stations and luncheonettes and just a few small-town banks. Their biggest take was $1,500. Their contemporary John Dillinger, who stole $74,000 in a single bank robbery, called them "a couple of punks" and complained that "they're giving bank robbing a bad name."

Yet Clyde Barrow and Bonnie Parker are more famous than Dillinger, perhaps more famous than any outlaws since Robin Hood and Maid Marian. Partly that's because of their Robin Hood–like reputation. It wasn't a reputation that they really deserved, since they preyed on rich and poor alike, and there's no evidence they passed on any of their haul to the latter. But it wasn't entirely undeserved either: they emerged from the ranks of the dispossessed during the Depression, and they saw themselves as striking back against a corrupt system.

As Bonnie wrote in "The Story of Bonnie and Clyde" (and her skill as a balladeer was itself one reason for their fame):

> *They call them cold-blooded killers*
> *They say they are heartless and mean*
> *But I say this with pride, I once knew Clyde*
> *When he was honest and upright and clean.*
>
> *But the laws fooled around and taking him down*
> *and locking him up in a cell*
> *'Til he said to me, "I'll never be free,*
> *So I'll meet a few of them in hell."*

What really made heroes of Bonnie and Clyde, however, was neither altruism nor poetry, but love—especially hers. From the time she threw her lot in with Clyde, Bonnie knew that it was likely they would die together, yet she never considered leaving him.

Bonnie's mother, Emma Parker, remembered pleading with her to give herself up before it was too late. "You'll get only a prison sentence if you come in now," she told her daughter in May 1933, with police across the country on the lookout for the pair. "And while that's bad, still and all, it's nothing compared to what may happen before this is over. You're not made for this sort of life, Bonnie."

But, as Emma Parker related it, Bonnie would hear none of this. "Clyde's name is up mama," she told her mother. "He'll be killed sooner or later, because he's never going to give up. I love him and I'm going to be with him till the end. When he dies I want to die anyway."

That was the way Clyde's sister, Nell Barrow Cowan, remembered it too. "Faced with the alternative of living as a law abiding citizen without Clyde's presence and love, or of going with him on his career of crime which eventually led to murder, she chose to go with him, live with him, and die with him," she said.

Or as Bonnie herself concluded her poem:

> *Some day they'll go down together*
> *And they'll bury them side by side*

> *To few it'll be grief, to the law a relief*
> *But it's death for Bonnie and Clyde.*

✦—✦

It was unfair of Nell Barrow Cowan to put all the blame on Clyde for leading Bonnie astray. True, Bonnie had been a good student in high school and never in any trouble with the law until she met Clyde. But in 1926, at the age of sixteen, she married Roy Thornton, a drifter who was soon arrested for robbery and sentenced to five years in the Texas prison system.

It's reasonable to assume, therefore, that when she first met Clyde, Bonnie was by no means appalled by his criminal record. Abandoned by Thornton, trapped in a dead-end job as a waitress, she was looking for a way out of the poverty of West Dallas. Clyde's ambitions, however criminal, were part of his appeal.

Not that Clyde was a particularly accomplished criminal. He'd started as a turkey rustler, then graduated to various petty burglaries and automobile thefts around the area. He was wanted in Denton and Waco when he first met Bonnie in January 1930 at a mutual friend's house.

The pair hit it off and—like any proper young woman—Bonnie invited him home to meet her mother. Emma Parker liked Clyde too, and she invited him to spend the night on the living room couch. "He was certainly a likable boy, very handsome, with his wavy hair, dancing brown eyes," she recalled. "He had what they call charm, I think."

Emma Parker was undoubtedly less impressed with her daughter's young man a couple of weeks later. Clyde was sleeping on the same couch in her house when the police arrived and hauled him off to jail.

Bonnie wrote to Clyde in jail, begging him to go straight. One letter went: "When you get out I want you to go to work, and for God's sake don't ever get into any more trouble." Another said: "Honey, if you get out OK, please don't ever do anything to get locked up again."

Clyde got off on the Denton robbery, but was found guilty on two counts of burglary in Waco and sentenced to two years in prison. Bonnie again wrote to him, declaring her love and saying she'd do anything to help him.

In March, before Clyde was to be transferred to the state prison, Bonnie visited him in the Waco jail. There she learned that he was happy to accept her help—in breaking him out. He told her the parents of a fellow inmate kept a gun in their house, and he asked her to break in, get the gun, and smuggle it into the jail.

"It's a way to get me out of here and us together sooner," Clyde explained.

So much for Bonnie's efforts to reform him. On March 11, she got the gun, hid it under her dress, returned to the jail, and slipped it to Clyde. That night, he used it to escape.

Bonnie and Clyde were now partners in crime.

◆•— —•◆

The partnership didn't seem destined to last very long. A week after the escape—before he'd even seen Bonnie again—Clyde was picked up in Ohio and taken back to Waco. This time the judge was less tolerant; he sentenced the young man to fourteen years in prison.

Clyde was assigned to the Eastham Prison Farm in Houston County. Police couldn't prove Bonnie's role in Clyde's escape, so she remained free. She continued to write him, though the letters gradually became shorter and less frequent. Bonnie went back to being a waitress.

In January 1932, desperate to get out of the hard labor at Eastham, Clyde cut off two toes on his left foot and was sent to the prison infirmary. Ironically, his parole came through two weeks later. After serving twenty months, he limped his way back to Bonnie.

A month later, Clyde and his accomplice, Raymond Hamilton, broke into a hardware store in Kaufman, a small town near Dallas. Bonnie, now a full-fledged member of the gang, acted as lookout.

But Clyde had not yet perfected his getaways. With the police in pursuit, the gang's car got stuck on a muddy road. The three burglars jumped onto some mules in a nearby field. Clyde and Hamilton managed to escape, but Bonnie was caught.

In jail, awaiting her trial, Bonnie had a chance to reconsider her life of crime. According to her mother, Bonnie promised never to have anything to do with Clyde again.

But a poem Bonnie wrote in jail, "The Story of Suicide Sal," indicated that even if Clyde had abandoned her, she would stick by him. The poem told the tale of a woman who, like Bonnie, had been left in jail by her accomplice and lover. It concluded:

> *If he had returned to me sometime,*
> *Though he hadn't a cent to give*
> *I'd forget all this hell that he's caused me,*
> *And love him as long as I live.*

In June, a grand jury found insufficient evidence of Bonnie's role in the Kaufman robbery, and she was released.

Meanwhile, Clyde had gotten himself into much bigger trouble. In April, while robbing a gas station in Hillsboro, a town south of Dallas, Hamilton had accidentally shot the store's owner. Clyde was now wanted for his role in the murder.

Still, Bonnie joined them in July, and the three committed various robberies in north Texas. In August, Clyde and Hamilton shot two Oklahoma officers who tried to arrest them for drinking (Prohibition was still in effect) at a dance in the town of Atoka. Now Clyde realized there was no turning back; after his role in the Hillsboro shooting, he might have gotten off with a long prison sentence, but after killing two sheriffs, he knew his capture meant a death sentence.

Whether Bonnie was there for the Atoka shootings is unclear. Some accounts say the trouble started when she rebuffed a local man's advances and Clyde came to her aid. Emma Parker said

Bonnie was home with her that night, and though she may have wanted to give her daughter an alibi, she didn't deny Bonnie's involvement in later murders, so it's likely she was telling the truth.

In any case, Bonnie didn't hesitate to rejoin Clyde and Hamilton after the shootings. Theirs was now a life always on the run, and it was during this period that they earned their reputation for daring getaways.

Clyde stuck to back routes, frequently stealing cars and changing license plates, but nonetheless constantly pursued by police. At the small town of Wharton, police blocked a bridge over the Colorado River. Bonnie and Clyde approached the bridge in one car, Hamilton in another. Although they were going seventy miles per hour, Clyde spotted the roadblock and quickly swung the car around. He and Bonnie then leapt into Raymond's car. Clyde took over the driving and left the pursuing police far behind.

Clyde's favorite stolen vehicle was a Ford V8, which was built to withstand his sprints along dirt roads and plowed fields. Clyde went so far as to write a letter of appreciation to Henry Ford himself: "I have drove Fords exclusively when I could get away with one," he told the automaker. "For sustained speed and freedom from trouble the Ford has got every other car skinned."

In April 1933, Bonnie and Clyde—now joined by Clyde's brother Buck, his wife Blanche, and a new gang member named W. D. Jones—hid out in an apartment in Joplin, Missouri.

Neighbors noticed them carrying a disturbing quantity of guns and ammunition into the apartment and called police, who surrounded the apartment. After a wild shoot-out in which two more officers were killed, the gang escaped.

Inside the apartment, police later found snapshots Buck had taken of the gun-toting couple, including one of Bonnie with her foot on a car bumper, a revolver in her hand, and a huge cigar in her mouth. The picture was soon printed in newspapers and magazines throughout the country, firmly establishing the legend of Bonnie and Clyde.

In reality, the gang rarely had time to eat or sleep, let alone pose for pictures. At one point, they stopped for a brief visit with Clyde's sister, Nell. (It was also a dangerous visit, since police kept an eye on their relatives.)

Nell asked Clyde where he was going next.

"He made an indefinite gesture," she recalled. "'Driving,' he said, 'Just driving from now till they get us.'"

Most accounts of Bonnie and Clyde focus on her love for him. That's understandable because she stuck with him knowing full well it was likely to lead to her death. It was hard to see Clyde as equally loyal, especially after he abandoned her amid the mud and mules near Kaufman.

But Clyde, if initially more selfish, became just as devoted and self-sacrificing as Bonnie. This became clear in June 1933 when, driving his usual seventy miles per hour, he crashed over the edge of a ravine between the Texas panhandle towns of Quail and Wellington.

The classic Warren Beatty–Faye Dunaway movie, *Bonnie and Clyde*, omits the accident completely, perhaps so Dunaway can remain beautiful to the end. But in fact Bonnie was severely burned and survived only because Clyde nursed her back to health.

Law enforcement officials taunted Emma Parker after the accident. They told her, she claimed, that "a man as hard, as cruel, as heartless as Clyde Barrow, will never put up with a wounded girl who is a dead give-away and a burden to him." They added that Bonnie would soon show up on some lonely road with a bullet through her head.

Not true. Clyde stayed by Bonnie's side, leaving Buck and W. D. Jones to carry out some robberies on their own. He fed her, changed her bandages, carried her to the bathroom, and did everything possible to make her comfortable.

"Many of the things they said of Clyde were true, but he had his code of love and loyalty," said his sister Nell. "Where Bonnie was concerned, Clyde was gentle as a baby, as tender as a mother. . . . During those last two years Clyde would have died a thousand deaths rather than to have hurt Bonnie."

Recalled Jones: "Bonnie was the only one Clyde trusted all the way."

Clyde's love for Bonnie seemed not to have been primarily sexual; in fact, many accounts, including the 1967 movie, portray Clyde as mostly impotent.

"Your advertising's just dandy," Dunaway's Bonnie says to Beatty's Clyde. "Folks'd never guess you don't have a thing to sell."

Other accounts claim Clyde was gay, and that Jones was both his lover and hers. There's no evidence to back up these claims. Jones himself, in a 1968 *Playboy* interview, explicitly denied them. "I've heard stories that Clyde was . . . as they say in the pen, a 'punk,' but they ain't true," he said. "Maybe it was Clyde's quiet, polite manner and his slight build that fooled folks. . . . I was with him and Bonnie. I know. It just ain't true."

Clearly though, what most turned on Clyde—and Bonnie— was not sex, but crime. This was the excitement they both craved.

◄•—•►

Bonnie and Clyde remained loyal not just to each other but to their families. In spite of the danger, they regularly snuck back to Dallas to visit.

According to Emma Parker: "We used every persuasion we could muster to get them to leave Texas forever, but they refused. 'Seeing you folks is all the pleasure Bonnie and I have left in life now,' Clyde said. 'Besides each other, it's all we've got to live for. Whenever we get so we can't visit our people, we might as well die and be done with it.'"

In the end, it wasn't their families but a fellow gang member who brought about their deaths. The beginning of the end came in January 1934, when the couple helped their old gang member Raymond Hamilton escape from Eastham, the same prison farm where Clyde had served. This was one of their most triumphant moments. But it also incurred the wrath of Texas officials, who brought in former Texas Ranger Frank Hamer to organize the efforts to capture the outlaws.

Hamer tracked down gang member Henry Methvin and offered a reduced sentence in return for setting up Bonnie and Clyde. On May 23, 1934, the couple slowed down on a road near Gibsland, Louisiana, when they spotted a man they recognized as Methvin's father. Hamer and his heavily armed posse, who were hiding behind an embankment on the side of the road, then pumped 187 shells into Bonnie and Clyde.

Clyde was twenty-five years old when he died, Bonnie twenty-three. Though they died together, Bonnie's poem erred in its prediction that they'd be buried together. Clyde was buried next to his brother Buck, but Emma Parker finally managed to separate Clyde from her daughter.

"He had her for two years," she said. "Look what it got her. He's not going to have her anymore. She's mine now."

24

Joe DiMaggio
and Marilyn Monroe

Theirs was a wedding surrounded by cynicism. How could it not be? The groom was the Yankee Clipper, generally acknowledged (at least in New York) as the greatest baseball player of his time. The bride was being promoted as "the next Jean Harlow," though her movies would soon far outgross Harlow's or anyone else's. The press had been gleefully awaiting the wedding ever since Joe and Marilyn first met in 1952.

"Will Mr. America marry Miss America?" wrote one reporter, "and if they split, who gets custody of the Wheaties?"

"Joe is looking over Marilyn Monroe's curves," reported another, "and is batting fine."

In spite of the hoopla building up to it, the ceremony itself was commonplace. There were no crowds—just a few of Joe's family and friends and none of Marilyn's Hollywood acquaintances. There was no church; Joe was a Catholic, but both he and Marilyn had been married before and the church did not recognize their divorces.

The wedding took place on January 14, 1954, in the judge's chambers of the San Francisco City Hall. The whole thing was over in less than three minutes.

But even in such a short period, even amid the inevitable hype that surrounds any celebrity coupling, Marilyn would introduce an ominously somber note. She carried three orchids throughout the ceremony. When they withered in her hand, her thoughts turned to death. She turned to Joe. If she died first, she asked him, would he place flowers at her grave every week—just as William Powell had done for Jean Harlow?

Joe promised he would.

❖

The cynicism could not be blamed entirely on the press. Both Joe and Marilyn, when they first met, had something other than love in mind.

Joe had first seen Marilyn in early 1952, in a photo where she posed sexily in a baseball uniform, pretending to be at bat. To him, she was just another pretty blonde, not so different from Dorothy Arnold, the showgirl who had been his first wife. Joe also thought—entirely wrongly—that the uniform she wore meant she was a fan, and that she might therefore be grateful for the chance to meet him. So he asked a friend to arrange a date.

Marilyn, who didn't think much of athletes in general, was reluctant. "I don't like men in loud clothes, with checked suits and big muscles and pink ties," she explained. But she was no dumb blonde, and she recognized a good opportunity. She also knew that some old nude photos of her were about to be released, and that these could present a public relations disaster. She calculated that being seen with the all-American hero might counteract that publicity, so she agreed to the date.

They met in March at a dimly lit Italian restaurant on Sunset Strip. Marilyn was immediately relieved to discover that Joe didn't wear pink ties, just a gray suit and gray tie. Joe was, it turned out, quiet and dignified—so quiet, in fact, that a friend once remarked when he said hello it was a long conversation. But this was fine with Marilyn, who found Joe a refreshing change from the fast-talking Hollywood types she was used to.

Soon the two were dating regularly, and they discovered they had a great deal in common. Both had been poor: he was the son of an immigrant fisherman, she had shuttled between foster homes and an orphanage as a result of her mother's mental illness. Both were suspicious, street-smart, and ambitious; both had remarkable bodies they'd used to get ahead, albeit in very different ways.

This relationship was clearly more than a publicity ploy; Joe and Marilyn were deeply attracted to each other, and not just physically. But a very practical streak remained throughout their courtship.

In 1953, Marilyn's career took off. *Niagara*, *Gentlemen Prefer Blondes*, and *How to Marry a Millionaire* grossed more than $25 million that year. Now Joe became her most trusted adviser. Consulting with her agents and lawyers, he proved that his years of negotiating with the Yankees had taught him as much about business as it had about baseball.

In January 1954, after negotiations with Fox broke down and the studio suspended Marilyn, Joe proposed. As Marilyn later described it, the proposal was decidedly unromantic: "One day Joe said to me, 'You're having all this trouble with the studio and not working, so why don't we get married now? I've got to go to Japan on some baseball business, and we could make a honeymoon out of the trip.'"

The wedding achieved a business purpose as well. Amid all the press attention, Fox caved in and reinstated Marilyn.

And the honeymoon, as Joe indicated, also doubled as a business trip. He appeared at some exhibition baseball games in Japan, and Marilyn joined the USO to entertain American troops in Korea. For four days in February, she toured Korea, singing for hundreds of thousands of soldiers.

Back in Tokyo, Marilyn excitedly told her husband about the shows. "It was wonderful, Joe," she said. "You never heard such cheering."

Joe thought a moment, then calmly answered, "Yes, I have."

It was a comment that could be interpreted two ways. On the one hand, it was a confirmation of all that Joe and Marilyn had in common, of their shared celebrity, of his genuine understanding of the joys and frustrations of stardom.

On the other hand, it was also a sign of a growing rivalry between the two. Joe was used to being the star, not the star's husband. During their honeymoon, the crowds were mobbing Marilyn, and Joe realized that his wife had become a bigger name than he was. He was brooding.

Worst, Joe wasn't at all happy about the nature of Marilyn's stardom. He most definitely did not like his wife being ogled by thousands of soldiers in Korea and millions of men back in America. This was not the way his mother and sisters behaved during his proper Old World upbringing, and it was not the way his wife ought to behave. He had married the sexiest woman in the world, but now it was time for her to become the sexiest housewife in the world.

Back in America, Marilyn tried. She told a reporter, "I like to iron Joe's shirts. I like to look at Joe in a shirt I ironed." But she admitted that her career didn't usually leave her much time to do the ironing.

More and more, Joe complained—about her revealing clothes, about the roles she played in movies, about the poses she took in publicity photos. Soon Joe, never talkative, didn't talk to her at all. When they were together, he would just stare sullenly at the TV, preferably set to a baseball game.

The crisis came to a head on September 13, when Marilyn— along with more than fifteen hundred spectators—showed up at Lexington Avenue at midnight. The crowd was there to watch the shooting of some publicity photos for her new movie, *The Seven Year Itch*. In the movie's most famous scene, Marilyn stands over a subway grating while the draft from a passing train lifts her skirt to knee level. The camera quickly cuts to Marilyn's face, which shows her grateful for the cool breeze.

But the crowd that night wasn't looking at her face. For two hours, they roared as, in take after take, her dress flew up, often as high as her shoulders, revealing a pair of thin white panties.

Joe didn't usually visit Marilyn at work, but he happened to be in New York, so at 2 A.M. he stopped by to pick her up. The director, Billy Wilder, recalled "the look of death" on Joe's face when he saw what was going on.

That night, other guests at the St. Regis Hotel heard angry shouting coming from Suite 1105-1106. Two weeks later—only six months after their wedding—Marilyn filed for divorce.

◄•—•►

The end of their marriage would not mean the end of their relationship. Once Marilyn was no longer his wife, Joe was less possessive, more genuinely supportive.

In 1960, after Marilyn broke up with her third husband, Arthur Miller, Joe was there, by one account showing up on her doorstep with a huge poinsettia plant. He saw her regularly after that, often sneaking in late at night and using the service elevator to avoid the press. No longer married, Joe and Marilyn were now genuinely close friends.

And Marilyn, more than ever, needed a loyal friend. In February 1961, depressed by the mixed reviews of her latest movie, *The Misfits*, and dazed by the large quantities of barbiturates she'd been taking, Marilyn checked herself into Payne Whitney, a mental hospital affiliated with New York's Cornell Medical

School. She expected a comfortable hospital room, a quiet place to recover.

Instead, she found herself locked behind a steel door with severely disturbed patients. And though she'd checked herself in, her doctors were unwilling to let her check out. This was Marilyn's worst nightmare; her mother had been institutionalized, and now she was too.

She called Joe in California, and he rushed to New York to rescue her. The doctors insisted Marilyn wasn't fit to leave, but this was Joe DiMaggio they were facing. He told them he was prepared to take the building apart brick by brick.

The doctors backed down. Marilyn was transferred to Columbia Presbyterian Medical Center—a hospital, but not a mental hospital. She was released three weeks later.

Did Joe and Marilyn ever consider remarrying? Accounts differ. Some friends of his say he planned to do so, that he always loved her. "He carried a torch bigger than the Statue of Liberty," said one close friend. Others conceded he still loved her, but said that he realized he could never live with her. Joe himself never said anything in public about it.

As for Marilyn, it seems unlikely she was ready to settle down with Joe. In the final years of her life, she had brief affairs with a number of other men, including—according to some reports—Frank Sinatra and John and Robert Kennedy.

Joe's most recent biographer, Richard Ben Cramer, said he'd proposed and she'd accepted, but Cramer doesn't attribute the story. In any case, it was definitely Joe who was Marilyn's most trusted and most valued friend. Sometime in early 1962, she wrote a note to him, saying, "Dear Joe: If I can only succeed in making you happy, I will have succeeded in the biggest and most difficult thing there is . . . Your happiness means my happiness."

She never sent the note. It was found in the Los Angeles house where she died of a drug overdose on August 5, 1962.

There has been almost as much written about Marilyn's death as about that of her reputed lover, John Kennedy. Indeed, some conspiracy theorists have linked the Kennedys to Marilyn's death. Some have argued they drove her to suicide by breaking off an affair, or more sinisterly, that they covered up some role in her death. Others have accused her doctor, her housekeeper, or the mob.

The most likely scenario remains that Marilyn killed herself, possibly by accident but probably not. There was a family history of mental illness. She had been depressed in the weeks before her death, especially after Fox fired her from a movie called *Something's Got to Give*. She was drinking too much and taking far too many pills.

In any case, it was Joe who, ever reliable, made the arrangements for her funeral. He barred all movie stars, studio executives, and press. (Among those who wanted to attend but were shut out were Frank Sinatra and Peter Lawford, an actor who was also a brother-in-law of the Kennedys.)

Just before the coffin was closed, Joe leaned over. "I love you, I love you, I love you," he said.

For the next twenty years, he had flowers placed weekly on her grave, just as he'd promised.